The Ladder of Influence

5 Steps for Climbing to the Next Level and Beyond

RIA STORY

WHAT OTHERS ARE SAYING ABOUT RIA AND HER BOOKS:

"I want to start by saying thank you…You made me want to try at life because you made me realize that you can make it anywhere you want, no matter where or what you are from. THANK YOU SO MUCH!"
JONATHAN, HIGH SCHOOL STUDENT

"Ria's book (Beyond Bound and Broken) is full of hope and inspiration, and she shows us that despite experiencing horrific trauma as a young adult, that if we choose to, we can get past anything with the attitude that we bring to our life…Her book is full of wonderful quotes and wisdom."
MADELEINE BLACK, AUTHOR OF UNBROKEN

"I am using your material to empower myself and my female clients. Thanks for sharing your story and a wonderful journey of growth."
SUE QUIGLEY, LICENSED CLINICAL THERAPIST

"Very few 'victims' would be willing to share such a personal story. However, nothing about Ria is average. She chose to rise above her painful past and now positions it in a way to offer hope and healing to others who've been through unspeakable abuse. Ria's faith and marriage keep her grounded as she reveals the solid foundation which helps her stand as an overcomer. Read this story and find yourself and your own story strengthened."
KARY OBERBRUNNER, AUTHOR AND FOUNDER OF AUTHOR ACADEMY ELITE, ON RIA'S STORY FROM ASHES TO BEAUTY

"Thank you, Ria, for bringing our conference to a close. You were definitely an inspiration to all of us! Awesome Job!"
MELINDA, PRESIDENT AGS

"*Beyond Bound and Broken is a deeply inspirational book; one that will stay with you for years to come. The lessons are deep, yet practical, and her advice leads to clear solutions. This is a profoundly hopeful book. We all face pain, difficulty, and doubt but with resilience, we can lead vital, flourishing lives. Ria's story although sometimes painfully difficult to read because of the trials she endured is a story of great courage and compassion both for herself as victim and for those who betrayed her. Forgiveness is a strong theme as is courage. I would highly recommend this book to anyone who is struggling to move forward after experiencing a great trial.*"
AMAZON CUSTOMER

"*…it was awesome! Ria has a real gift. I came away with so many helpful tools! Thank you, Ria.*"
STEFANIE, CONFERENCE ATTENDEE

"*May God continue to bless your efforts. Your triumph is a great joy, and a gift to all that would hear or read it.*"
LOUIS O., HUMAN RIGHTS ADVOCATE

"*What an inspiration you are to all of us especially the women audience. Your book is a clear example & step by step guide on how to become an effective leader. It is so easy to read and simple yet meaningful which is the beauty of this book.*"
K. POONWALA, CUSTOMER SUCCESS MANAGER, ON LEADERSHIP GEMS FOR WOMEN

"*I was truly inspired by your presentation and the life lessons taught.*"
JENNIFER, CONFERENCE ATTENDEE

See more testimonials at:
riastory.com/testimonials

For those who have the courage to climb
to the next level and beyond.

CONTENTS

INTRODUCTION

We all want, and at some level need, to be successful in life.

Regardless of whether we are a CEO of a multi-billion dollar organization, a mid-level manager in a small company, or a front-line associate, we want to be successful at what we do. And, we want to be successful at influencing the people around us at home, at work, and within our circle because, let's face it, life gets better when we have more influence with other people.

When we have more influence with other people, we get more opportunities. When we have more influence, we have more options. When we have more influence, we have more choices.

Life will always be better with more options, more opportunities, and more choices.

Influence is one of the most profoundly complex, and at the same time, incredibly simple concepts. We all have some influence, yet we all want more influence. Simple. But who, how, where, when, and why we influence as well as how we in turn are influenced by others is incredibly complex because people are incredibly complex. Situations are different. People are dynamic. Relationships are complicated.

For example, we can't influence our boss the same way we influence our children. (We would never attempt to bribe our boss the way we bribe our children to get them to behave in the grocery store!) We may not be able to influence our next-door neighbor in the same way we would influence our mother. We can't influence our teammates the same way we influence our spouse.

And, we can't influence anyone else in the same ways

as we influence *ourselves.*

In 2008, I read my first real "leadership" book. It cracked open a door to the brand-new-to-me concept of influence being a skill **I could develop** instead of being a trait I was either born with or born without.

That book helped me understand **we all have the ability to increase our influence and how much better our lives will be when we do.**

The Ladder of Influence represents 5 Steps we can use to climb as we strive to reach the next level and beyond, personally and professionally. What will this book mean to you? Only you can answer that. Maybe you are dreaming of a better relationship with your kids. Maybe you are dreaming of more influence and more options in your career. Maybe you are dreaming of both of these things and much more.

I want you to dream of "something better" because that dream is the inspiration and starting point for change. As Amy Tan said, *"We dream to give ourselves hope. To stop dreaming, well, that's like saying you can never change your fate."*

Most of the time, "something better" is possible. The question is, are you committed to putting in the work to achieve it? In other words, are you willing to sacrifice what is necessary to make your dream a reality? Hope starts with dreams, but you must put in the work to turn your dreams into your reality.

As Colin Powell stated so well, *"There are no secrets to success. It is the result of preparation, hard work, and learning from failure."*

Any time you are climbing, effort and work will be required. You will struggle at times. Trust me, no one ever accidentally ended up on top of Mt. Everest. Climbing the Ladder of Influence will require energy, focus, time, and dedication, as you invest into yourself, your future, and your success.

If you are looking for shortcuts, there aren't any. This isn't a "get rich quick" book, or a "become a 7-figure sales person in 7 days" program you can enroll in for just $99. This isn't a "get skinny, popular, and successful in 12 steps" video series.

This is a road map, a guide. When using any road map or guide, you must still do the traveling yourself. I can show you the steps, but you must do the climbing.

The steps I'll be sharing are principles. And, much like gravity always applies (at least, here on earth!), the principles here will always apply. I will also be sharing some practical application tips for increasing your influence both at home and at work. These applications are my suggestions based on my experience but are simply that: suggestions. You know your situation best, so take my suggestions, use what you can, and don't be afraid to think beyond what is in this book. If you find yourself struggling, revisit the principle and consider a different way to apply it. There are many ways to apply and benefit from a principle.

Along the way, there will be detours. You will encounter challenges. You will make mistakes. But, the beauty of a journey without end is there is no timeline. You may climb as fast or as slow as you choose.

The key is to keep climbing. Much like driving across the country, you cannot see the entire journey ahead before you begin. But, if you drive to the first bend in the road, you will be able to see a bit farther. And, as you drive a bit more, you will see a bit more.

Stay your course. Keep going. Keep growing. Keep learning. And above all, keep climbing.

Chapter One

THE LADDER OF INFLUENCE

"Influence is ultimately an outcropping of trust - the higher the trust, the greater the influence."

~ Dale Carnegie

The Ladder of Influence provides a powerful, yet simple framework to help you realize the practical steps you can take to increase your influence with the people around you: friends, family, followers, co-workers, your boss, team members, community members, children, spouses, and maybe even ex-spouses too!

There are three truths you must know:

1) **You can't change anyone except yourself.** This isn't a book about how to change others, fix others, or make other people listen to you. This is a book about accepting responsibility for what you can change. And then, having the courage, making the choice and taking the action to do so. Most of the time, you can increase your influence with someone. However, you must stop blaming them and start working on what you can change – yourself.
This is not easy to do. The reason we blame other people is it's easy. If it's "their fault," then we don't have to do anything to improve the situation. We blame others because there is only one alternative. The moment we stop blaming others is the moment we must accept responsibility. Humans naturally want to externalize blame. But, that doesn't serve us. What if we always believe it's up to the other person to change the situation, but they never do? The greatest limiting belief is the victim mindset.

Playing the victim will not take you forward in life. Playing the victim won't help you be successful. Playing the victim won't allow you to realize your potential, fulfill your purpose, or achieve your goals. Avoid the victim mindset at all costs. You cannot change everything, but you always have the power to change yourself. Find the courage to change yourself, and develop the wisdom to understand that changing yourself changes the world. *Your* world.

2) **There will be people you simply cannot influence.** These people do not share your values. Perhaps that near-retirement, fussy, been-there-forever person you work with isn't interested in being influenced by a 30 year old with new ideas. They simply aren't going to change, for you or anyone else, because they don't value growth, change, or seeing things "get better."

Perhaps the fairly new, young front desk associate you hired won't read the personal growth book you recommended to her, although she won't stop complaining about not being promoted quickly enough. She simply doesn't value sacrificing her Netflix-every-night habit to invest in her own development. You will be able to influence most people, but there will be a few who don't want your influence. Don't hate them, blame them, or fight them. They are heading in a different direction in life. It's their life, and they get to choose the path they will travel.

Stay positive, stay true to your course, and keep climbing. You may be surprised one day to discover you've gained influence with them simply because you refused to give up on doing the right thing and staying positive.

3) **You will never stop climbing.** That's because you will be at different places at different times in different relationships. You may climb to the fourth step in one relationship. Then, you meet someone new and have to start again at the bottom as you begin developing that relationship. There are five "steps" on the Ladder of Influence. You will find yourself striving to climb to different levels at different times with different people. And, just like a real ladder, you can't skip steps. On a real ladder, you must use the step below to climb to the one above. You cannot stand on the third step of a ladder until you've climbed past the second step. Even in long term relationships where you have achieved a certain level of influence, you must never forget that your influence was built from the ground up – and with every interaction, you must remember to start with the bottom step, *Control of Self.*

If you fall off the Ladder and lose all influence, you may be able to rebuild the relationship but only by going back down to step one and starting again. And even then, you may not be able to repair the relationship. Relationships are built on trust, and trust is like an egg. Once dropped, it's difficult to put Humpty Dumpty back together again without some permanent damage. Remember, relationships should never be taken for granted.

Chapter Two

WHY A LADDER?

"When you increase your influence, you increase your options."
~ Mack Story

Influence is incredibly dynamic. You can obtain some influence simply from having a title or position of authority such as manager, owner, or police officer. But, this type of influence is limited, because people who follow you because they "have to" only do what they "have to." In this book, I will focus primarily on authentic influence – that is, influence based on who you are as a person, how you interact with people, and the relationships you have with others.

Why do I use the framework of influence as a ladder? To begin with, it's clear there are different degrees of influence. I use the framework of a Ladder because the degrees of influence stack on top of one another.

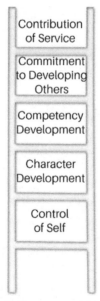

You can build influence with people around you

simply because you are proactive and have *Control of Self*, or you can lose influence if you don't. This is easier to understand when you consider the following. I bet you've never lost your temper, yelled at someone, and thought, "I think they'll like and trust me more now!" Or, have you ever had someone get mad and blame you for something, and you trusted them MORE as a result? Most likely, the answer to this question is no.

As time passes, your *Character* will strengthen or weaken relationships. For instance, you'll generally have much more influence with your spouse than you will with someone you have just met. However, if you have developed a bad relationship with your spouse, you may not have a lot of influence in that relationship either.

You will also develop a certain amount of influence based on your *Competency*. For example, if you are excellent at your job, have a reputation as being an expert, or perhaps have become highly skilled after years of gaining experience, you'll have a degree of influence with someone who comes to you for help at work.

If you've ever had a trusted mentor pour into you for an extended period of time, they likely had a high degree of influence with you. Perhaps they took time to mentor you, counsel you in difficult times, or gave you good advice. They built a high degree of influence with you based on their *Commitment to Developing Others* (namely, you).

Someone like Mother Teresa still has tremendous influence long after her death, even with those she has never met. She has influence based on her *Contribution of Service over Time*, the highest step on the Ladder of Influence.

You move to a higher degree of influence as you climb higher on the Ladder. And, you can't simply jump to the top step. You must start climbing from the bottom. This applies whether you are in a professional environment at work or a personal environment at home.

Authentic influence is based on relationships which are determined by character and values. In other words, relationships are built on trust. The more trust you have in the relationship, the more influence you will have.

Developing trust takes time.

Developing a high degree of influence takes time.

It's important to note that influence can be positive or negative. There are, and have been throughout history, some powerful influencers who used their influence in negative ways. Hitler for example. The difference is whether influence is used to manipulate and control or to motivate and inspire others to achieve positive results.

Remember, my focus in this book is to help you develop *authentic* influence which is based on who you are as a person. I'm not concerned with the amount of *artificial* influence you may have because of your title, position, rank, or a specific situation.

To truly develop your influence and leadership as a person in a position of authority, I highly recommend a book written by my husband Mack Story, "*Blue-Collar Leadership & Supervision*®." Even if you don't consider yourself "blue-collar," the content will be relevant.

Of course, I'm biased because I'm married to him. But, his book explains how to excel at leadership and influence as a person with a title or position far better than most "leadership" books I've read. Download free excerpts from this and most of his other books at BlueCollarLeadership.com/download. No email required. No subscription or registration. No signing up for a spammy sales pitch or newsletter. Just another resource we provide to help you climb.

Chapter Three

CLIMBING THE STEPS

"The supreme quality for leadership is unquestionably integrity. Without it, no real success is possible."

~ Dwight Eisenhower

You must start at the bottom of any ladder in order to climb to the top. The Ladder of Influence is no different. You must start at the bottom step, *Control of Self.* And, you must do the climbing. No one else can do it for you. No one else *will* do it for you.

How high and how fast you want to climb is up to you. However, be careful as you climb. You can easily slip and fall. It may take only one mistake because with people the little things are often the big things.

Your influence is built over time by your choices, words, actions, and interactions. With every word, action, and interaction, you are either building influence with those around you and climbing higher up your ladder – or you are decreasing influence and slipping back down. Each interaction is making a deposit into or taking a withdrawal from the "trust" account of the relationship.

When it comes to influence, who you are matters. What you say matters. But, what you do matters most because who you are on the inside determines how you do what you do.

For example, if you tell someone you will meet them at 10:00 am but don't show up until 10:30 am, they may forgive you. But, they won't trust you as much as they did before. They now know you can't be counted on to keep small commitments, and you don't value their time.

If you have a strong relationship with them based on much trust built over time, one incident may not be a big deal. But, it will leave a negative impression relative to your character and who you are as a person. Do you take your word seriously or not? Are you a person who can be trusted to keep a commitment or not? Of course, life happens. But, a pattern of making and breaking commitments will cost you influence. And whether you realize it or not, it can be very expensive, difficult, and sometimes even impossible to regain influence that has been lost.

Someone who has climbed higher on the Ladder of Influence will have higher standards relative to integrity, respect, and influence in relationships than someone who has not climbed as high.

When you meet someone, you'll likely have a blank slate. Your choices, words, actions, and interactions will determine what's written on it. Sometimes we don't think about it, but small things such as the way we dress for an appointment can affect our influence. Do you take pride in your appearance? I don't mean you must "dress up" all the time, but do you take time to make sure you are neat, clean, and your physical appearance is appropriate relative to those you most want to influence?

You will usually have very little influence with someone you've just met – unless they have heard about you, heard you speak, or perhaps read about you. What they know about you in advance will increase or decrease your influence.

In situations like this, your influence may increase as they get to know you, and you meet or exceed their expectations. Or, your influence may decrease if you don't measure up.

I once met an author who had co-written a very popular series of books. I was writing my first book, so I was interested in meeting this author. They had some influence with me because I had read their books and heard about them.

However, quickly after meeting them, they started losing influence with me. They didn't demonstrate a high degree of *Control of Self*. This person lost control of their temper in a very public situation, while speaking on stage. Their poor character was revealed to me and everyone else in the audience. They hadn't begun to truly climb the Ladder of Influence.

In general, it's possible to have some influence based on a level of *Competency*. Someone who has been successful with their career certainly can have some influence based on their success. However, if influence isn't built first on *Control of Self* and then *Character Development*, it's not based on moral, authentic, high level influence.

If you have a great job and make lots of money but you can't control your temper when things go wrong, you will never be able to develop the highest levels of influence.

Perhaps someone built a successful business but ran over people, abused their team members, took advantage of others, or even cheated their way to success, it will become evident over time. They can't hide who they are for very long. The higher *you* have climbed, the quicker you will be able to tell if someone else has also climbed or if they are trying to shortcut their way to the top.

If you value taking advantage of people, you can build influence with someone who shares your values. You may be able to influence someone who doesn't have a high degree of character, but that won't take you very far in life relative to developing a high level of influence.

There are no shortcuts when it comes to influence. If you haven't truly started at the bottom of the Ladder of Influence and climbed the steps based on your *Control of Self*, *Character*, and *Competency* (the first three steps), it will quickly become evident to those who have. You won't be able to truly influence others who have a high degree of character.

Chapter Four

FIRST STEP: INFLUENCE BASED ON CONTROL OF SELF

"Hold yourself responsible for a higher standard than anybody expects of you. Never excuse yourself."

~ Henry Ward Beecher

The first step on the Ladder of Influence is the *Control of Self* step.

We all have an "inner two-year-old" living inside us. Humans have a natural tendency to want to respond to the world around them and everything that happens in their world based on the emotions they have in the moment. That's normal, but responding based on emotions in the moment generally doesn't serve us well. Andy Stanley reminds us, *"Your feelings can be terrible leaders."*

When you were literally two years old, you may have expressed frustration, discontent, or anger by diving to the floor and pitching a temper tantrum. You may be able to get away with that behavior at two but not likely at 30. As Stephen R. Covey tells us, *"When something happens, human beings have the freedom to pause and choose their response."*

The choices we make mentally and physically in response to what happens to us (stimulus) are critical because they will impact our situation, positively or negatively, short term and long term.

When you choose the right response based on your values and what will serve you best, instead of choosing a response based on the emotions of the moment, you will likely increase your influence. When you don't choose the right response, you will likely be decreasing your influence to some degree.

We've all gotten it wrong, and we've all gotten it right. The key is realizing we *can* control ourselves and when we do, we climb higher on the Ladder of Influence.

None of us are going to be perfect in life. Climbing the Ladder of Influence isn't about being perfect. It's about accepting responsibility when we make a mistake and learning how to improve in the future.

The four dimensions of life are: 1) the heart dimension (spiritual or faith based; where our values are chosen); 2) the head dimension (mind, emotional intelligence, personal growth, and thoughts); 3) the health dimension (our physical body and environment); and 4) the social hierarchy dimension or relational area (where we see the impact of our influence with others). *Control of Self* is related to all of them.

The interesting thing is: The choices we make in the first three dimensions determine most, if not all, of our influence in the fourth dimension, social hierarchy.

Control of Self relative to whether you spend your free time developing yourself in some way or binge watching Netflix will have an impact on your influence. Sure, it's more "fun" to sit around all day watching TV and eating Cheetos, but that won't move you very far forward in life. You may increase your influence in some small way with others who binge watch Netflix, but you won't be increasing your influence with those who don't place a high value on that activity.

If you've never invested time developing yourself, you will not be able to build much influence with someone higher than you on the Ladder of Influence because they value personal development.

When you lose control of yourself, regardless of how or why, you are losing influence in some way. You may not realize it's costing you opportunities or influence, but it is.

Losing your temper at work may cause you to miss out on a future promotion or raise. Losing your temper with your young children when they make a mistake may cause you to lose influence with them in their teen years.

Because mastering *Control of Self* is foundational to

personal and professional success, this is the first step on the Ladder of Influence.

Control of Self shows up in many areas: setting your alarm clock, so you won't be late for work; having the discipline to exercise, so you stay healthy; staying organized, so you aren't late for meetings; controlling your emotions when things go wrong, so you don't damage relationships; and so much more.

Two-year-old moments look different for different people.

Remember, *Control of Self* means more to those who are ahead of you on the Ladder of Influence. Someone who doesn't value their health won't care if you smoke 10 packs of cigarettes a day. But if your boss values healthy living, even though they won't expect you to make the same choices they make, you will lose some measure of influence with them if they know you smoke a pack a day.

The words you use and what you talk about demonstrate what you value which affects your influence. Can you control your words? Do you use profanity?

Your behavior affects your influence. Are you the same person at home? At church on Sunday? At work? At the tailgate for the big game?

When it comes to influencing others, you must realize your choices will make you or break you. In terms of influence, the question isn't whether your choices are "right" or "wrong." The question is, "How are those choices impacting my influence?" The next questions you should answer are, "How high do you want to climb?" and "What do you need to change in order to reach that level?"

Chapter Five

CLIMBING TO THE
FIRST STEP

"Emotional self-control is the result of hard work, not an inherent skill."

~ Travis Bradberry

When we begin to realize everything impacts our influence with others (and even with ourselves), it becomes apparent there are no small decisions in our day to day lives. Anything compounded over time will have a big impact, so it's crucial for us to be intentional with our values, thoughts, decisions, choices, words, and actions. It's crucial, *if* you want to get somewhere specific in life and *if* you want to be successful. If you're content to simply live a mediocre life, this book isn't for you. Climbing is hard work. It's challenging. But, it will always be worth it.

Climbing to the first step on the Ladder of Influence is perhaps the most challenging for two reasons: 1) It's the first step. The first step is always the most difficult because you don't yet know how to do it, and you are seldom great at something the first time you do it; and 2) It's easy to get discouraged because you haven't developed a pattern of success yet. Creating change in any dimension of life is hard, creating positive changes relative to *Control of Self* requires humility, reflection, intentional thought, and commitment to change. It will also require you to intentionally raise your level of self-awareness.

Let's start with the first dimension. *Control of Self* relative to the heart dimension is more about actually spending time deciding your values and then living them out. For example, if you've made the decision to value going to church because of your religion, then *Control of Self* will be living that value out by going to church. If you value caring about other people, then *Control of Self* will be behaving in ways that demonstrate to other people that you do care about them. That may be volunteering, tithing, or giving to charity. It may be mentoring someone. You alone get to decide how that value should be lived out in your life – but then, you must live it out.

Emotional/Mental *Control of Self* in the head dimension is where the challenge increases. There is nothing wrong with having emotions. We are human, and humans have emotions. Emotions are physiologically triggered responses based on hormones, neurological connections in our brain, conditioned responses, past experiences, and our thoughts.

Often, our emotions are created based on the *thoughts* we have about what is happening to us currently or what has happened to us in the past. Sometimes, it's the story we tell ourselves about *why* something happened that creates the strongest feelings. Regardless of whether the stories we tell ourselves are true or not, they can stir up powerful emotions. Next, we make a choice based on those emotions. That choice causes us to take action. The action impacts our situation and creates our circumstances.

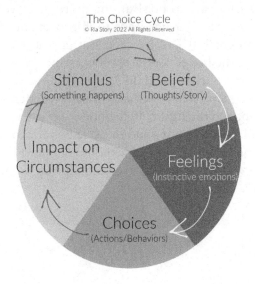

The Choice Cycle
© Ria Story 2022 All Rights Reserved

Stimulus (Something happens)

Beliefs (Thoughts/Story)

Impact on Circumstances

Feelings (Instinctive emotions)

Choices (Actions/Behaviors)

We must strive to align our beliefs, thoughts, and stories with reality. Then, we must make emotional choices that benefit us. Better choices will lead to better behavior which will improve our circumstances and cause something positive to happen. I refer to this as the Choice Cycle.

Emotions steer you. Choices determine you.

You can always choose to be proactive and respond to anything that happens to you in life based on what you value most and what you feel will move you forward. If someone says something you don't like, you can choose to value being positive and respond with kindness instead of anger. If you get sick, you can choose to appreciate what's good in your life instead of focusing only on your bad health.

Being proactive means you accept what you cannot control (other people, much of what happens to us, etc.) and focus on what you can control: yourself, your emotions, your choices, and your actions.

This isn't easy to do. But, the more often you do it, the easier it gets. Practice leads to improvement. No one will get it right 100% of the time, but the more often you get it right, the better your life will become.

Reflect on what you didn't get right in the past. Then, start making small changes that will lead to better results in the present and the future. Remember, you have the ability to control your emotions and to make better choices.

No one can control you without your permission.

Control of Self is the key to a better life, at home and at work.

Chapter Six

THE FIRST STEP
AT HOME

"Self-control is one mark of a mature person; it applies to control of language, treatment of others, and the appetites of the body."
~ Joseph B. Wirthlin

The essence of *Control of Self* is being able to lead and influence *yourself* in a way that allows you to increase your influence with others personally (at home) and professionally (at work).

For most people, it's easier to control themselves at work or in public. But when they are at home, they let their emotions boil over onto the people they love the most. For example, some people struggle to forgive their ex-spouse, and their bitterness costs them influence with their teenage children. Others may lose their temper when their favorite team loses. Unfortunately, for many the battle isn't emotional, it's physical.

Perhaps it's unfair, but the reality is: The choices we make about our physical health can also impact our influence.

I once took a fitness class where the instructor talked throughout the class about making good food choices as well as regular exercise. However, this individual was clearly overweight and struggled to get through the workout. I'm not at all judging this person for being overweight because we all fight different battles.

But, she didn't inspire or influence me based on that interaction because she is clearly still struggling with *"Control of Self"* with respect to her health habits. That's totally okay – her physical goals, choices, and actions are hers. I'm certainly not blaming her for them. My point is to remind you that choices, especially compounded over time, have consequences. Those consequences can be positive or negative. Good or bad, your physical or health related choices will impact your influence.

Having *Control of Self* physically means being able to control our choices, habits, and physical actions just like having control of our emotions. Sadly, we often use emotions as an excuse for behaviors that don't serve us. "I've had a bad day/week/childhood/life, so I deserve (or need) _____." Fill in the blank with anything from ice cream, to drugs and alcohol, to buying something you can't afford while telling yourself it's retail therapy. Almost any behavior can work against us if we are: 1) doing too much of it; and/or 2) engaging in it as a way to numb our emotions.

Remember, the question (relative to influence) isn't really "Is this right or wrong?" but rather, "Is this moving me forward in life and helping me climb the Ladder of Influence?" Once you understand what you truly value, behaviors that aren't moving you forward should become easier to let go of. I wrote much more about behaviors and habits in my book, *Fearfully and Wonderfully Me: Become the Woman You are Destined to Be.* (It's filled with principles that are relevant to men too!)

Here is a checklist to help you focus on *Control of Self* in specific areas at home:

☐ I have a personal growth plan, or I am actively developing myself on a regular and consistent (daily/weekly) basis. *(Reading personal growth/leadership books, listening to personal growth/leadership audiobooks or podcasts, watching personal growth/leadership videos)*

☐ I consistently practice applying what I'm learning. *(Identify principles to apply in specific situations.)*

☐ I am regularly reflecting and learning from my mistakes. *(What went wrong? Why? What will I do differently next time to achieve a better outcome?)*

☐ I have resolved, or am working to resolve, any issues from my past that impact me negatively. *(Trauma, childhood adversity, military service, sexual violence, etc.)*

☐ I am aware of my emotional triggers and stay away from situations that provoke me to think, feel, or behave in negative ways. *(Which situations cause you to lose control? Choose to avoid them when possible.)*

☐ I respond proactively to my family, even when I'm stressed/hurt/angry/sick. *(Pause, breathe, and take control of emotions before speaking. Respond based on the importance of the relationship long term, and your feelings __for__ others, rather than what they said or did.)*

☐ I accept responsibility for my thoughts, the stories I tell myself, my choices, words, and actions in response to what happens at home. *(I do not make excuses. I don't blame others for my responses and choices.)*

☐ I am intentional with my physical health: eating, exercising, resting. *(I intentionally focus on my health and keep my indulgences at healthy levels.)*

☐ I keep commitments to my spouse, children, family and friends. *(I don't make promises I can't keep. If I say I will do something, I do it.)*

Chapter Seven

THE FIRST STEP
AT WORK

"I have learned that I really do have discipline, self-control, and patience. But they were given to me as a seed, and it's up to me to choose to develop them."

~ Joyce Meyer

When it comes to *Control of Self*, it's generally easier for most people at work than it is at home. It's a bit ironic that the people we love the most often see us at our worst while the people we work with usually see a more "filtered" version of us. That's because we usually have stronger emotions when it comes to our home life. We care more, therefore we are more emotional. And, it's much more difficult to control these stronger emotions.

However, it's still just as important to make sure you have developed *Control of Self* at work and are able to be proactive with your boss and co-workers too.

Whether we have a boss or own a business, we all want more influence professionally. The key is realizing the choices we have made, are making, and will make, are either increasing or decreasing our influence with the people we work with or do business with. Influence is built much like a cathedral – one brick at a time.

Those who don't have *Control of Self* at work may be angry with their boss because they didn't get a raise or get the promotion they thought they deserved. Others can't get along with a co-worker and think "it's their fault." Others aren't happy with their current job, but they're still blaming someone else for their circumstances. They're all frustrated and losing influence.

Work ethic and ability to control our emotions relative to the work itself and the people we work with is either helping us climb the Ladder of Influence or holding us back.

The biggest opportunity for having *Control of Self*

relative to work comes when change happens. People don't like change (unless it was their idea). And when change happens, most people waste time and energy complaining about it and thinking of reasons NOT to change, instead of embracing the opportunities change brings. Mack and I published a book, *"Change Happens: Leading Yourself and Others through Change,"* to help others proactively deal with change. If you struggle with change personally and/or professionally, you may want to check it out.

The second biggest opportunity to increase your influence at work through *Control of Self* is to become more valuable to others (developing yourself) and intentionally adding value to everyone around you. Go the extra mile, do more than you have to, do it before you have to, do it better than you have to, share information, and help others, especially your boss, and you'll be successful.

Here's a checklist to help you with *Control of Self* at work:

☐ I accept responsibility for my career choices. *(My choices brought me to where I am today.)*

☐ I actively control my emotions at work. *(My goal is to build trust, so I pause, reflect, and think before speaking or acting with co-workers, in meetings, with clients, etc.)*

☐ I show up on time for work and meetings. *(And, I make sure to prepare for the day or meeting in advance.)*

☐ I finish on time and keep commitments to my boss, teammates, clients, and others within the community. *(I don't make promises I can't or won't keep. If I say I will do something, I do it.)*

☐ I respond to emails, messages, and phone calls within 24 hours. *(Even if I can't address it right away, I acknowledge receipt of the email or message.)*

☐ I go above and beyond when supporting others. *(I realize if I want to become more valuable, I must deliver more value.)*

☐ I realize I'm working for myself, and my work ethic is impacting my influence. *(I don't complain to co-workers or customers, and I am fully engaged.)*

☐ I embrace change. *(When change happens, I focus on shining instead of whining.)*

☐ I do the things my boss doesn't like to do. *(I realize my boss is my number one customer!)*

☐ I take initiative and give my best effort. *(I realize if I can't be 100% committed to the team, then I should find a different team.)*

☐ I don't complain about my co-workers or my boss. *(I focus my energy on what I can control.)*

☐ I don't hoard information, and I freely share information to help the team/client be successful. *(I realize the most valuable player makes other players valuable.)*

☐ I maintain a positive attitude at all times. *(I don't pretend there are no problems, but I look for the positive in every situation.)*

Chapter Eight

MASTERING THE
FIRST STEP

"The people you surround yourself with influence your behaviors, so choose friends who have healthy habits."

~ Dan Buettner

Being proactive is a challenge for all of us at times. Life is hard. Life isn't fair. Things go wrong. Someone cuts us off in traffic. The waitress puts our order in wrong at the restaurant. People say or do things we don't like. Our emotions are going to bubble up, sometimes unexpectedly.

Being proactive and having *Control of Self* is more than being able to control emotions, thoughts, words, and actions. It's also about accepting responsibility for yourself, the choices you made in the past, and reflecting on the choices you need to make *now* to create the future you want.

Want better health? Start making better choices relative to your health. Want a bigger salary? Start making better choices relative to your career. Every choice you've ever made has brought you to where you are today. Of course, there will be circumstances outside of your control. But in each of these circumstances, you must choose how you deal with them, positively or negatively.

Have you ever read one of those "you choose the story" books where you choose what the character will do next at the end of each chapter? Your choice will determine which chapter you read next. Throughout the book, there's a choice to make at the end of each chapter, so you have a say in how the story goes.

I never liked those books. I always wanted to go back and read how the story would have gone if I had chosen differently for the character. I wanted to "do it over" and see how it could have been.

Sometimes, we can look back on life and see where things could have been different. Sometimes, we'll never fully know what impact our choices in the past have had. But, we don't get to do it over. That's life. The important thing is that we accept responsibility for our choices (good or bad), stop blaming anyone else for where we are today, and start taking control of our life.

Once you have mastered the first step on the Ladder of Influence, you will start to realize in your everyday interactions when others aren't "there yet." Have patience with them, share the principles you have learned, and help them begin to climb the Ladder of Influence. Not only will it help them increase their influence, it will also help you increase your influence with them. It will also make life (yours and theirs) better because there will be less turmoil.

You will also start to realize most of the drama people have in their lives is avoidable and most stress is self-induced. When you have *Control of Self*, you realize that it really doesn't matter what happens externally, you are the one who controls your emotions internally.

Someone recently called me for advice on how to handle a work situation with a co-worker. Her co-worker essentially sexually harassed (verbally) her, and when she reported it to her supervisor and HR, it was brushed over and ignored by the leaders within the organization.

"You have three options," I told her. "1) Quit your job. Culture is based on leadership and won't change until leadership does; 2) Keep working there and be miserable about it, blaming the organizational leaders because they won't address it or stop it. You can become angry because it happened, bitter because it was tolerated, or frustrated because you'll still be working with this person."

She didn't like either of those two choices.

I continued. "Or…3) Keep working there and control your emotions. Regardless of what the person said, you have a choice to let it make you upset and angry, or not.

It's not right that they said it, but you don't have to choose to let it make you mad. Don't let it ruin your day, week, or life."

Please understand, I'm not endorsing harassment or any other action where someone wrongs us. I think the leadership of that organization is failing miserably because behavior like that is permitted. My point is she had a choice to let the drama and emotion of the moment roll over her or to let it roll past her.

It's a powerful concept, but not an easy one to master. Life happens. Problems occur. Challenges arise. People do or say things we don't like or that aren't right. But, the choice of how we respond is entirely up to us. And the more you get it right, the easier it becomes to get it right.

Start small. Start by exhibiting *Control of Self* when little things happen. Forgot your umbrella? Don't blame someone else for not reminding you. Learn to set your umbrella by the door, and be grateful there wasn't a tornado.

What happens to us is not as important as who we become because of it. I left home at 19 to leave behind a father who started sexually abusing me at age 12 (and later trafficked me) and a mother who blamed me for it. I left home with a duffle bag and a pillow case filled with some clothes. No matter what happens in life, you can be bitter about it or become better because of it. It's your choice. My choice is to become better.

You don't build much influence by having *Control of Self* when things are going right. People pretty much expect you to control your inner two-year-old when everything is going your way. It's when things are falling apart and you demonstrate *Control of Self* that you have the opportunity to increase your influence with others.

Chapter Nine

SECOND STEP: INFLUENCE BASED ON CHARACTER DEVELOPMENT

"No one else has as much influence in your life as you do."

~ Ria Story

The steps on the Ladder of Influence are stacked one on top of the other, like a real ladder. Therefore, it's possible to place one foot solidly on the *Control of Self* step while also placing the other foot on the next step, *Character Development*. There will always be room to improve at every level, so we should never stop working to master the steps below as we strive to climb to those above.

Character is about more than being "good" or "bad." Character is all of the qualities and values that make up who we are. Who we are determines what we do and how we do it. Our character also determines why we choose to do the things we do.

Who we are determines much of our influence in both personal and professional relationships.

To some degree, having *Control of Self* means we have done some work on "who we are" already. *Control of Self* is the private side of our character. Now, let's discuss the public side of our character – how people experience who we are.

When developing our character, we are essentially choosing to think at a higher level. How we think will dictate what we do, how we do it, when we do it, and ultimately who we will influence.

Character Development is similar to growing taller. We see the world from a different perspective if we are looking at it from a greater height. In other words, if we were a child standing 3' tall, we couldn't see over a 4' tall fence. But once we grew past 4' tall, we would be able to see what's on the other side. It was there before, but we didn't know it because we couldn't see it. But now, we have a new perspective. The unknown has become the known.

As we develop our character, we develop our thought patterns and improve the quality of our thinking. Improved quality of thinking is going to translate into improved quality of choices, actions, and results – especially related to our relationships.

We all have strengths and weaknesses of character just like we all have strengths and weaknesses of competency. In terms of increasing influence, we should focus on developing **weaknesses** of character and **strengths** of competency.

Developing weak areas of competency will never allow us to be more than average in that area. For example, I'm not a very talented singer. I could spend the next 20 years developing my singing skills, but I'll never have as much influence as a singer as someone who is a naturally gifted singer. That's okay, there are many other areas I am naturally competent in, and I can develop more influence in those areas because I naturally have a head start. So, I focus on developing my strengths relative to competency.

But, our character weaknesses hold us back the most.

In Chapter 3, I mentioned how a pattern of being late for appointments can create distrust, and therefore decrease influence in relationships. Being late is a sign of character weakness. Maybe, it's a lack of planning? Maybe, it's a lack of discipline and waking up on time? Maybe, it's a weakness relative to managing your daily activities? Maybe, it's something else? But, being late reveals we cannot lead ourselves well relative to our schedule. Trust will be lost. Influence will fade.

If you are always late to work, your boss isn't going to be able to depend on you. If you are always late to pick up your children from school, your character weakness will impact how they feel about you and how much they trust you.

Failing to lead yourself well within your schedule will hold you back in life in terms of influence even if you don't realize it. Remember, character development is like being taller. Those with a higher degree of character will see what you don't. Your weaknesses will appear bigger to them.

Think of it this way. Would you trust someone more or less if they always keep their commitments to you? More of course. Everyone else feels the same about you.

Keeping commitments is a character trait. All of your character traits (good and bad) determine who you are as a person. Each of these traits and characteristics can be changed or enhanced to increase your influence.

It won't happen immediately. Building trust and influence takes time. As you begin to develop your weak areas you will start to strengthen relationships and have more influence as time passes. If you were frequently late to work in the past, but develop your character enough to start always showing up on time, you will slowly begin to rebuild trust and increase your influence with your boss.

Being late is one simple example. Some other areas of character weaknesses that hold many people back include: arrogance (inflated sense of self), callousness (lacking empathy), stubbornness (unwilling to change, learn, or listen), dishonesty (deceit), vanity (pride), pessimism (always seeing the negative), hypocritical (saying one thing but doing another), manipulative (using other people), temperamental (moody or volatile), malice (intentionally hurtful), prejudice (preconceived opinions), indecisive (won't make decisions), impatience (unwilling to wait), and even the common "bad" habits that reveal character.

This is by no means a complete list, just some qualities to reflect upon as you consider what traits may be holding you back and which components of your character you want to target.

Chapter Ten

CLIMBING TO THE
SECOND STEP

"Personal transformation won't be quick or easy, but it will be worth it."

~ Ria Story

Character can change over time with growth, but it's not going to change very much from day to day. Who you were yesterday isn't likely going to be any different from who you are today. But if you have been intentional about growth, who you are today will be dramatically different than who you were five years ago.

To get different results, when it comes to influence, we must develop ourselves. And for many of us, the thought of dramatic change can be scary.

Don Miguel Ruiz, Jr. said it this way, *"When we place ourselves in a safety zone where we feel comfortable and secure and we are firmly entrenched in the this-is-who-I-am mindset, the worst thing imaginable is that it will all go away."*

Ask yourself the following three questions. When you can answer yes to all three, you are ready to climb to the second step on the Ladder of Influence:

1) The **Reality** question: Am I dissatisfied with my current reality?
2) The **Mindset** question: Do I believe it can get better?
3) The **Value** question: Do I value growth more than I value remaining the same?

The first question is easy. Many people aren't satisfied with their current reality. The second question is more difficult. Sometimes, we have limiting beliefs and may not even be aware of them. Belief drives behavior. If you don't believe it, you won't work to achieve it. Go back and review Chapter 5 if you struggle with belief.

The third question is where the going gets tough. Most

people want improvement, but many don't want to make the required sacrifices.

What this looks like when it comes to character development is an intentional growth plan. There can be several elements to incorporate into your growth plan: reading/listening to personal growth books, listening to leadership podcasts, watching personal growth videos, journaling, thinking, writing, etc. Regardless of which elements you prefer, you must intentionally build them into your daily schedule.

You may have to sacrifice something in order to do that. Maybe it means giving up some streaming time? Maybe it means getting up earlier? Maybe it means spending your money on resources that will help you? You must decide what is most important in your life, and you must decide what you are (and are not) willing to sacrifice in order to get it.

To be highly effective at developing your character, you must make daily growth a habit. This may look like reading one paragraph a day of a book on a related subject. It may look like listening to one podcast a day while you drive to work. It may look like 10 minutes of your morning routine being dedicated to reading a leadership book.

You will find a list of recommendations and resources in the Resources Appendix to get you started.

You don't always have to be taking big steps forward, but you must be consistently stepping forward. Joe Castillo said, *"Direction and destination can be planned before setting out, but the days of the journey are measured by how often the traveler strays from the path."*

You must be committed to growth because there will be days when you don't "feel" like putting in the effort. Do it anyway. If you've truly mastered *Control of Self,* your feelings will no longer dictate your actions. Leverage the discipline you've developed to grow on the days when you don't feel like reading or learning.

Learn something every day. Then, try to apply what you're learning every day. Share what you're learning with others. Try to apply it at work and at home. Reflect upon what worked, what didn't work, and why. Think about how you can achieve better results next time.

As time passes, *Character Development* will begin to impact the quality of your thinking – and therefore the quality of your life. Once you begin to master *Control of Self*, you'll be prepared to tap into the power of being intentional about *Character Development*. You'll discover you are intentionally writing the story of your life one choice at a time.

Being intentional about your choices allows you to live on purpose in each dimension of life, which will directly impact your ability to influence the people around you. As you change who you are, you'll also change what you're capable of doing because your abilities are a natural result of your values, thoughts, and emotions.

Being intentional about *Character Development*, means you get to choose how, when, and how much you will grow. Life can and will challenge you. However, the adversity and problems you face will provide new opportunities for growth. You may have heard of post-traumatic stress. Well, I'm a big fan of post-traumatic growth. In other words, you grow by overcoming adversity.

You must reflect on the past while actively searching for the positives that came from the experience. They will always be there – if you are willing to search for them. As Viktor Frankl said best, "*When I can no longer change a situation, I am challenged to change myself.*"

Chapter Eleven

THE SECOND STEP
AT HOME

"Resistance to change is proportional to how much the future might be altered by any given act."

~ Stephen King

When it comes to climbing the Ladder of Influence, consistency beats intensity every time.

It's the same for weight loss. For instance, if I want to lose five pounds, I may decide to exercise. I go to the gym, exercise for an hour, and get on the scale. But, my weight hasn't changed. I go back to the gym the following day, work out for another hour, and discover my weight still hasn't changed. I'm making progress, but it's not noticeable to anyone yet.

Many people would get frustrated at this point and quit. But, we should consider two things: 1) Successful growth (change and transformation) is a process; it takes time to produce results; 2) Progress will begin before we start to see results. The key is to stay the course and push past the "point of no results."

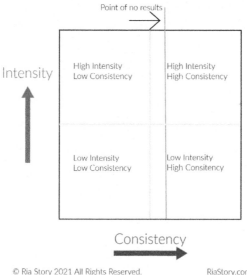

RiaStory.com

To climb, you must be consistent. Reading one book during your lifetime isn't going to lead to consistent growth. You can't master anything if you only do it once. You certainly can't master developing your influence if you aren't willing to sacrifice the time and energy to do so.

Remember, influence is established through relationships. Relationships are built on trust. To increase your influence, you must strengthen relationships by creating more trust. To do that, you must avoid taking withdrawals from "relational trust accounts" while making sure you're being intentional about making deposits.

When it comes to climbing to the second step on the Ladder of Influence at home, you can't fake it. The people you live with, have personal relationships with, and spend the most time with are likely to see the worst side of you. Your character can be masked, but it can't be hidden.

Who you are on the inside determines how you interact with people on the outside, especially the people you are closest to. They will experience your character in many situations: when you are sick, when they are sick, when you are happy, when you are healthy, when you are upset, when you are broke, when you are struggling to help an elderly parent, when everything is going well, etc.

Here is a check list for you to use when working on *Character Development* at home:

☐ I am aware of my natural personality traits. *(Am I naturally outgoing or introspective, more withdrawn or more aggressive, task-oriented or people-oriented, etc.?)*

☐ I am aware of my spouse/significant other's natural personality traits. *(How do my natural personality traits clash or mesh with theirs?)*

☐ I am conscious of my "Love Language" and my spouse's "Love Language." *(I help them understand what makes me feel cared for, and I frequently and intentionally "speak" in my spouse's Love Language.)*

☐ In my personal relationships, I take responsibility for what I can control. *(I own my mistakes and focus on improving myself rather than attempting to "fix" others.)*

☐ I do not complain about my spouse/significant other publicly. *(If I have a concern, I address it privately.)*

☐ I add value to those around me at home. *(I help them, before they ask for help. I am generous with my time and attention. I do things that prove I care.)*

☐ I value the relationship more than being right. *(I respect the other person, even when we disagree.)*

☐ I practice empathic listening regularly. *(I completely listen with my full attention, reflecting back what is being said, acknowledging feelings, and seeking to understand the other person's perspective.)*

☐ I have healthy boundaries for personal relationships. *(I don't hesitate to change or end toxic relationships.)*

☐ I reflect upon the mistakes I've made in personal relationships. *(I apologize quickly when needed. I make sure I do everything possible to avoid repeating the mistake.)*

Chapter Twelve

THE SECOND STEP
AT WORK

"Never let your competency be higher than your character."
~ Jason Denam

The irony of climbing to the second step on the Ladder of Influence at work is that it doesn't start at work. It shows up at work, but it starts at home. Most of the time when you're at work, you're busy doing your job. Your best opportunity to study character development content is going to be when you're not at work because that's when you have discretionary time to develop yourself.

It's unfortunate but true. When an opportunity appears, it's too late to prepare. Many people miss out on opportunities at work because they aren't willing to put in the time and invest in personal development up front. The key is to prepare for an opportunity before it arrives. Then, when it shows up, you'll be ready for it.

You've already learned the importance of a regular and consistent growth plan. That can be as simple as your commitment to learn something every day. It doesn't have to be complicated – you simply must do it. Would you think differently next year if you learned one new thing every day this year? Would you be more valuable?

The same character-based principles that help you improve personal relationships will also help you increase your influence in professional relationships. While you're learning how to more effectively listen to your children or spouse at home, you'll also be learning how to be a more effective listener at work. If you're growth-oriented on the weekends at home, you'll likely become growth-oriented during the week at work.

Of course, some resources are more relevant to work. See a list of my recommendations for professional development in the Resources Appendix.

Much of your growth will happen when you aren't at

work. But, there are some things you can focus on while at work to accelerate your climb.

Adopt the attitude and mindset of becoming a helper. Walk in the door every day determined to shine, help your co-workers, boss, and customers. Make sure you over-deliver on your projects. Don't make commitments you can't keep. If you can't deliver the results, don't make the promise. If you don't know the answer, don't pretend you do. But, don't let that stop you from finding the answer.

Always make sure you are acting with integrity. If the organization or your leaders don't value and model integrity, that's a sign you need to find a new work address.

Henry Cloud said, *"Character is the ability to meet the demands of reality. Integrity is the courage to do so."*

I love his definition of character and integrity because to meet the demands of your reality, you will definitely need the right amount of character. And sooner or later, staying true to your values will require courage.

Make a habit of helping others solve problems, over-delivering in all areas, being the most valuable team player by making the most players valuable, and watch your influence soar as your relationships at work improve.

☐ I maintain a file with all my professional development records. *(I keep a list of books read, training sessions attended, etc., and **I'm prepared to talk about what I've learned from each.**)*

☐ When I attend a conference or training session, I intentionally take notes to share. *(I purposefully pay attention and share what I've learned with others on my team.)*

☐ I regularly add value to my peers at work. *(I go above and beyond when asked for help, or I offer to help before I'm asked.)*

☐ I volunteer for new projects and roles. *(I understand that having more experience makes me more valuable.)*

☐ I look for ways to prevent problems from occurring. *(I'm always looking for solutions to existing problems or issues too.)*

☐ I listen respectfully in meetings when someone else is talking. *(I listen first and share my thoughts second.)*

☐ I don't attempt to take credit for things that went well. *(I prefer to give credit instead of taking credit.)*

☐ I don't blame others when things go wrong. *(I take responsibility for what I did or didn't do, could have done, and should have done.)*

☐ I intentionally build good relationships with my team members. *(I know about their families, hobbies, or any celebrations or challenges they may have.)*

☐ Most often, I focus on people first and tasks second. *(I connect with my team before going to work.)*

☐ I lead or participate in regular growth and development sessions at work. *(I attend/lead book study groups and/or podcast discussion sessions etc.)*

Chapter Thirteen

MASTERING THE
SECOND STEP

"To do something you've never done, you have to become someone you've never been."

~ Kyle Wilson

How do you know what you look like? I'm sure anyone reading this book has seen photographs of themselves or their reflection in a mirror. But, that's only going to reveal what you look like physically. What do you look like emotionally? Spiritually? Ethically?

Do you appear one way when others are watching and a different way when no one is watching? Are your words and your behavior the same when you're with your family, at work, at church, with friends, or in traffic?

What character traits do you value? Would the people you know best say you model these traits consistently? Often, our biggest blind spot is the one between us and the mirror. Stephen R. Covey said it well, *"We judge ourselves by our intentions and others by their behavior."*

We often struggle to identify our character weaknesses. Or, we know what they are but minimize the importance of developing them. Your character will launch you or limit you. Which will it be? It's up to you.

The quality of our choices reveals the quality of our character.

Character Development isn't easy, but it is necessary if you want to continue climbing the Ladder of Influence. Who you are determines how you interact with the people around you. Who you are determines the choices you make and the actions you take. Every choice you make will either maximize or minimize your influence.

John C. Maxwell reminds us, *"Your character growth determines the height of your personal growth. Without personal growth, you can never reach your potential."*

In my book, *Fearfully and Wonderfully Me: Become the*

Woman You are Destined to Be, I use the analogy of character being like a tree. When a tree is only a little seedling, it's easily pushed over by others. Its limbs are easily broken. It can be uprooted completely without much effort, and a minor storm can do major damage.

Think of your character as a tree. When you're young and naive, it's easy for other people to push you around, mold you, manipulate you, and hurt you because your character isn't fully developed.

But over time, if a tree is nurtured, it grows taller and stronger. It puts down strong roots, and those roots bring nutrients to the leaves. As the tree grows, some of the small limbs may be broken, but the trunk becomes stronger and can withstand many strong storms. As long as the tree is growing, it's getting stronger. But when it stops growing, it begins to wither and weaken.

When it comes to growth, your character is like a tree.

I love this analogy for character because it's visual. Your values are the roots which ground your character and help you stand firm in the storms of life.

We must choose the right values and have the integrity to live in alignment with them. That's why our choices, habits, and the influence of those around us are so critical. Every moment is a *defining* moment when you realize every moment is shaping your "tree" in some way.

The people around you are helping you grow, or they're not.

What you're reading, watching, and listening to is helping you grow, or it's not.

What you think about is helping you develop your character, or it's not.

What you spend your spare time doing is helping you reach your potential, or it's not.

The great thing is you don't have to get it right all the

time. You simply must ask yourself, "How can I get better today?" Then, take action based on your answer.

The key to mastering the second step isn't having character because everyone already has some degree of character, either good or bad, positive or negative. The key to mastering *Character Development* is intentionally doing something daily to improve your character. Once you've made personal growth and *Character Development* a habit, you are definitely standing strong on the second step of the Ladder of Influence.

As you grow and develop your character, your ability to evaluate the character or lack of character within others will increase.

It's important to understand you will be drawn to people who share your values. If you value being proactive, you will naturally want relationships with people who are proactive. If you value being reactive and playing the blame game, you will be attracted to those who do the same.

If your values cause you to make different choices in life, do different things with your time, or spend your energy in different ways than you did in the past, you'll likely have to leave some people behind. You'll notice some relationships begin to fade. This is a natural result of the growth process. This isn't because you are "better" than anyone. It's because you're choosing to move in a new direction, and they're not. You can still love them or care about them while spending less time with them.

Mastering *Character Development* means you've mastered taking responsibility for yourself and stopped blaming others for your circumstances. You focus on what you can control and influence which increases your influence with others. As time passes, you'll notice your influence with people of high character increases.

Chapter Fourteen

THIRD STEP: INFLUENCE BASED ON COMPETENCY DEVELOPMENT

"We are what we repeatedly do. Excellence then, is not an act, but a habit."

~ Aristotle

Once you master the first two steps on the Ladder of Influence, you will discover climbing to the third step is relatively easy, because the third step is all about your competency: talents, abilities, skills, and knowledge.

Influence at this level comes from being exceptional, being highly productive, getting amazing results, and making things happen. Those who are very task focused enjoy developing their influence at this step because it comes naturally and easily to them. Climbing always takes work, but once you master *Control of Self* and *Character Development*, you will have the discipline and dedication to develop your competency.

When you climbed to the second step, you focused on developing your character weaknesses. At the third step, you will focus on developing your competency strengths. Developing your strengths at this step is where you will really begin to shine and be noticed.

For this reason, it's important to be aware of your strengths. What are you naturally good at without much effort? Work on developing these areas. What are you not good at doing? Don't spend much time developing these areas beyond what is necessary to know at a basic level. The best you can hope for here is average.

For example, if you aren't good at reading after a lot of effort, but you are great in math with little effort, work on developing your math skills because you can become exceptional in math. If you aren't gifted in reading, you could spend 10,000 hours developing your reading skills and potentially still be below average relative to those who are naturally great. Beyond the basic reading skills you need for life, you shouldn't spend much time worrying about development in this area. Focus on development relative to your gifts and natural talents, so you can shine in your strength zone like the star you are meant to be.

Self-awareness is important and so is the ability to recognize your strengths and weaknesses. When you realize where you are strong, become laser focused in that area. When you realize areas of weakness, make sure to team up with someone who is strong in that area or delegate those tasks to others who will perform well.

Mack and I do this a lot. We are very different and have different strengths when it comes to competency. So, we divide our business related tasks accordingly. I'm naturally task-focused. Mack is naturally people-focused.

When we arrive at an event to speak, I start getting us set up and ready to make things happen. I check to make sure our water bottles are filled, our book racks are set up and filled with books, etc. Mack is always more focused on shaking hands and meeting people. That's okay, I like to shake hands and meet people too – I just like to set up the books first! Because we understand each other, it's easy for us to work together and leverage our strengths.

Once you have pinpointed your strengths, you will be challenged to define excellence for yourself in those areas. No one gets excited about mediocre or average results. Do you remember who the 20th ranked NFL, NBA, or MLB team was last year? No one else does either. But, a lot of people remember who finished in 1st Place.

Your goal should be to relentlessly develop your competency strengths, so you can claim a 1st Place trophy in the game of life. The key is aligning your energy with your strengths, so you can establish a track record of consistently delivering exceptional results.

Exceptional means you go above and beyond what is

required. Exceptional means you don't settle for the status quo. Exceptional means you leverage the minor details in major ways. Excellence builds confidence. Confidence builds trust. When you can demonstrate you are not only competent in an area but also exceptional, you will build more trust with more people.

More trust equals more influence.

Something else to consider is making sure you know precisely where your talents, passion, and purpose overlap. You may be good at many things. But if you aren't excited to be doing those things, you will never have as much influence in that area as someone who is.

Identifying your passion and purpose takes time. Some great resources to help you in this area can be found in the Resources Appendix. You should also spend some time reflecting on the things you are great at and love doing. Things that people are willing to pay you to do.

You must have passion to make great things happen. When you make great things happen, you build momentum both personally and professionally. Momentum is your best friend when it comes to building influence at this step on the Ladder of Influence.

Influence at this step increases because you start making things happen, not because you talk about making things happen. Henry Ford said, *"You can't build a reputation on what you are going to do."*

One of my key insights was realizing activity and accomplishment aren't always related. In other words, being busy does not necessarily equal being productive. I generally find it easy to be busy. I became much more effective when I stopped spending my time and energy on things that didn't move me forward relative to my goals or to my purpose…helping others develop themselves.

Chapter Fifteen

CLIMBING TO THE
THIRD STEP

"Nothing builds self-esteem and self-confidence like accomplishment."
~ Thomas Carlyle

One of the first, best, and most important keys to learning to climb to the third step on the Ladder of Influence is to learn to say no. Saying no to the wrong things, the unimportant things, the things of lesser value, the things you shouldn't be doing, the things you don't do well, the things you aren't called to do, and the things that are more of a priority for someone else, will give you the space, time, and energy to say yes to the right things.

When you are good at making things happen, you are going to get asked to make a lot of things happen. Other people are going to ask you to help make things happen – things that may or may not be on YOUR list of priorities. And, if you aren't willing to tell them no, you will find yourself spending more time on other people's projects or priorities than your own. Don't fall into this trap, make sure you graciously say no with a smile because you are laser focused on where you are gifted and called.

There are three key questions you must ask and answer to begin mastering the third step and significantly increasing your influence at this level:

1) **The Principle Question: What must I do?**
   This question prompts you to examine the tasks, projects, and things on your "to-do" list and remove what is unnecessary relative to your roles and responsibilities in life (and/or leadership). For example, if you chose to have children several years ago, you now have a role as a parent and a responsibility to those children. You can't simply get rid of them. Or, if you choose to work at an organization, you will have certain job related

responsibilities. And if you want to keep your job, you must do what's required of you to fulfill your part of the employment agreement.

Of course, you must do what you have to do. But, make sure you are crystal clear on what that is. Many times, we do things we don't truly "have to" do. We simply choose to do them while complaining that we are too busy. If you find yourself saying, "I don't have time to _____ ," then it's time to examine your values, priorities, and calendar. You are the only one who can control your time and energy, so take control.

My book, *PRIME Time: The Power of Effective Planning,* is dedicated to this topic if you need additional help. In it, I introduce you to values-based living and time management principles.

2) **The Passion Question: What do I love to do?**
This one may be easier to answer. What are you driven to do? What do you want to do? What are the activities that bring you the most joy when you do them? What do you love doing so much that you would be happy to do it for free? What keeps you thinking instead of sleeping? What do you dream of doing that you're actually capable of doing? What gives you satisfaction? What are the problems in the world that break your heart? If you could only do one thing in life, what would it be? If you could only help one person in life, who would it be? The answer to these questions will help you define and refine your passion which will lead you to your purpose.

3) The Purpose Question: What should I do?

This question prompts you to focus on developing competencies specifically related to your purpose. Some people know early in life what their purpose is, while others must work hard to figure it out as they go. Where do you feel called to contribute? When what you're good at intersects with a definite need that must be met and you feel fulfilled, you will find clues related to your purpose. You may discover this overlap at work or at home.

Experiences shape us. Often, people want to give back to others who are walking a path similar to their own. Your purpose might be serving customers in your business, raising your children, becoming the best team player at work, or solving a major problem in the world. You get to choose. Your purpose will naturally evolve over time with intentional growth as you narrow your focus.

15 years ago, I thought my purpose was helping people become their best self through my role as a group fitness instructor. I loved every minute of it! Today, I help people (primarily women) become their best self by helping them increase their influence, develop leadership, and maximize their results in life. I make my greatest impact through writing and speaking as I help people overcome the mindsets, self-limiting beliefs, choices, and habits that are holding them back. I've simply become more centered in the area of my gifts and calling.

Once you have answered these three key questions, you should have a pretty clear idea of where what you are gifted at doing overlaps with where you are called and what you love to do. But, you aren't done yet. Keep climbing!

Chapter Sixteen

THE THIRD STEP
AT HOME

"A successful life is a series of successful days. Your daily habits are creating your future."

~ Jim Collins

When it comes to increasing your influence at home relative to *Competency Development*, it's more about getting results *in your role*, than it is about excelling in any one area.

You will find it much easier to increase your influence at home when you have some measure of stability, organization, and personal success. Chaos in the home rarely, if ever, helps you increase your influence.

Influence at this level is enhanced by accomplishment because you can't give someone what you don't have. You must be successful as an individual to increase your influence based on competency.

For example, you're not likely to be effective teaching your children how to develop and use a budget if you haven't learned how to do it yourself. You will struggle to get them to save their money if they have been watching you spend your money on things you really don't need. Or, you won't likely be able to help your family eat healthy if you haven't learned and modeled eating healthy yourself.

It's also important to make sure you have time for the important things in your life at home: relationships. You could be the most successful CEO in the nation. But to influence your spouse and children at a high level at home, you must be home.

Remember, authentic influence is based on relationships; relationships are built on trust. To build trust based on a specific competency, you must be able to deliver results consistently in that area. You must also ensure you are focusing on what's important to those in your family. Focus only on doing what's important to you, and you will be creating distrust with your family members.

Bill Hybels reminds us, *"Your schedule should not be based on what you need to do, but rather on what you want to become."*

Personal success at home will look a little different for everyone based on their specific values and goals. The important thing is to be a healthy, whole, fulfilled, principle centered individual who is committed to personal growth. Growth doesn't always mean moving on or moving up. Sometimes, growth means becoming the best person you can be right where you are.

Consider what you need to do in light of your role in the family or household and make sure you do it well. If your responsibilities include laundry then keep the laundry done or drop it off at the laundromat or the dry cleaner. If you usually take care of cutting the grass, make sure it gets done. Take responsibility for managing the things you need to manage whether it's your checking account, your living space, or your work/life balance.

You will find your influence decreases when you cannot or do not close the gap between expectations and reality.

☐ I make sure to protect time in my schedule for my personal relationships. *(I rarely or never miss important events and celebrations. I set aside quality time for my relationships daily.)*

☐ I am clear on what I can do to add value to my spouse, and I make sure I do it. *(We discuss division of chores, how we can help each other in our strengths, etc.)*

☐ I keep my word when I make promises to my children. *(If I say we will do something Saturday, we do it; if I say I will pick them up, I do it.)*

☐ Relative to competency, I know what my personal definition of success is, and I'm intentionally working toward it every day. *(I am regularly developing my competencies in areas relevant to my role at home.)*

☐ My personal goals are aligned with my personal growth. *(I set and achieve goals, yet still continue to grow.)*

☐ I take on only what I can handle and remain in harmony with my personal life. *(I say no to other people's priorities when I need to; and I help my family do the same.)*

☐ I finish what I start. *(I make sure to get results when I set out to accomplish something.)*

☐ I am organized. *(I know what's important to me, my spouse, and my children/family. I make sure to keep track of the important things.)*

☐ I have time for the unexpected. *(I am flexible when needed.)*

☐ I make deposits in my personal relationships instead of demands. *(I go first when it comes to doing something for others instead of waiting for them to do something for me.)*

☐ I focus on what I can do to improve relationships, instead of nagging others about what they need to do to improve. *(I realize I cannot control anyone, but I can increase my influence by focusing on myself.)*

Chapter Seventeen

THE THIRD STEP
AT WORK

"Too many people sit around realizing their limitations when, maybe, they should spend more time realizing their potential."
~ Erik Weihenmayer

Climbing to the third step at work is almost exclusively about your ability to get results, make things happen, and excel in your areas of focus.

When it comes to getting results, I've already covered the importance of keeping commitments, meeting deadlines, and completing projects. If you want to increase your influence at work, you must start by making sure you meet expectations for getting the work done. Not your expectations – your leader's or customer's expectations. That's the baseline, or the minimum acceptable level, for getting results. You must do the minimum required to keep your job. However, you can't stop there if you want to keep climbing the Ladder of Influence.

When it comes to making things happen, you absolutely need to make things happen for yourself at work. But to be highly effective, you must help other people make things happen. Helping your co-workers be successful must also be a goal. Share your knowledge, your skills, and be willing to develop others.

Many people won't teach or train others, because they're afraid of someone taking their job. In truth, if you are continuing to develop yourself, you will always have more value to add. When you have more value to add, you are more valuable. It's a paradox, but when you try to work yourself out of a job, you almost guarantee you will never be without a job.

When it comes to excelling in your area of focus, you should strive to be seen as a subject matter expert who has a depth of expertise. It's been said that a "jack of all trades" (someone who tries to do everything) is a master of none, and they won't have a high degree of influence based on competency. To have a high degree of influence based on competency, you must have a high degree of competency. This won't happen unless you have a high degree of focus. Focus on your desired area or field. Then, master it. Be the best at it. Become the expert who continues to grow, and few, if any, will ever catch up to you.

Think about it from your perspective. If you need heart surgery, would you rather have a specialist who has performed thousands of heart surgeries or a general surgeon who has only done a few? You would want the specialist of course. Now, apply that logic to your competency at work. Focus creates value.

When possible, avoid working in your weak areas. It's not always possible, there will be some job related tasks you simply must do, even if you don't enjoy them or aren't excellent at them. But over time, try to move toward your interests and especially your area of focus.

Know what you are good at, and do more of that to master the third step at work.

- ☐ I know what is required of me at work, in my job, or in my business. *(Relative to what I do, I know what the minimum requirements are to be successful.)*

- ☐ I go the extra inch or the extra mile to deliver on a project. *(I go above and beyond what is required.)*

- ☐ I don't take shortcuts when it comes to quality, safety, or service. *(I don't compromise on excellence even when no one else will know.)*

- ☐ I am self-aware relative to my competency strength zone and my weak areas. *(I know what I do really well.)*

☐ I spend at least 80% of my working time in my high-leverage strength zone. *(I avoid spending much time on tasks I am not good at.)*

☐ I spend at least 5% of my time intentionally developing my competency strengths. *(I am regularly developing my areas of focus relative to my competencies.)*

☐ Relative to all the things I am good at, I am continually narrowing my area of focus. *(I am honing my skills in fewer areas but at a greater depth.)*

☐ I am training my replacement at work. *(I am continually developing or mentoring someone to take my place.)*

☐ I ask for help when I need it. *(Because I value the success of the team overall, I'm quick to reach out for assistance.)*

☐ I share knowledge, specialized expertise, and wisdom from my experience. *(I don't withhold information from my team.)*

☐ I welcome feedback, ideas, and suggestions from others. *(I'm always seeking improvement and open to ideas on how I or my team can get better.)*

☐ I respectfully answer questions at work, even when I think the answer is obvious. *(I am not sarcastic, nor do I belittle those who don't know as much as I do.)*

Chapter Eighteen

MASTERING THE THIRD STEP

"Until we dedicate time each day to developing ourselves into the person we need to be to create the life we want, success is always going to be a struggle to attain."

~ Hal Elrod

The key to mastering influence at the third step on the Ladder of Influence is, much like the previous two steps, dependent on continued growth and development. Not because there is anything wrong with us, but because we can always get better. Michael Josephson said it best, *"You don't have to be sick to get better."*

Why wouldn't we want to get better? When we get better, our family gets better. Our work gets better. Our life gets better. Our community gets better.

Our *world* gets better when we get better.

Deep inside, most people want to get better. Most people want to grow, do work they find fulfilling, and reach their potential. However, only proactive people will follow through and make it happen. Only proactive people take responsibility for their lives and refuse to embrace a victim mindset.

Until someone says, *"I am here because my choices brought me here,"* they haven't really taken responsibility.

Eleanor Roosevelt once said, *"I am who I am today because of the choices I made yesterday."* That means, who (and where) you want to be tomorrow is based on the choices you make today.

Many people will settle in life both personally and professionally because they aren't willing to grow, sacrifice, get outside their comfort zone, reach for something, take risks, or fail forward. These people will never realize the benefit that comes from living life intentionally.

Mastery happens daily, not in a day. Just as planting seeds today won't provide fruit tomorrow, you won't see results after one day or even several days.

Be careful which seeds you are planting. Plant growth and development seeds by learning, reading personal growth or leadership books, listening to great podcasts, developing your skills, etc.

In time, you will harvest the fruit from those seeds.

You don't plant orange seeds expecting an apple tree to grow. You don't plant poor choices and receive positive results in your life. It's a law of nature. You shouldn't blame others for the seeds you have planted. But, you can plant better seeds and, in time, have a better harvest.

Don't believe me? Start making poor choices and watch how quickly they begin to affect you and your life.

Beyond continued development and making wise choices, become a master of making things happen. Get results for yourself, your family, your organization, and help others do the same. The greatest plan or strategy in the world is worthless without implementation.

Successful people have a natural tendency toward taking action. They get frustrated by sitting around talking about something when they could be out making it happen. So, they go out and make something happen.

Sometimes, they can be too aggressive which can lead to mistakes or ruptured relationships.

Highly effective, successful people realize they need to balance relationships with the need to get results. There are times when you have to push, and push hard. But if it's done with respect for others, you can still achieve the objective while maintaining solid relationships. This is why it's crucial to avoid skipping steps as you climb the Ladder of Influence. Why? Because character leverages competency. What you do is important. But when it comes to influence, how you do it is more important.

Regardless of your level of success, highly effective

influencers know they must treat other people as people, rather than objects. John Holmes stated this beautifully when he said, "*It is well to remember that the entire universe, with one trifling exception, is composed of others.*" Don't make the mistake of thinking anyone else is less important than you. Don't sacrifice long-term relationships to make short-term gains.

Here are some things that will stop you from mastering the third step. Make sure to avoid:

- Procrastination (putting things off)
- Making excuses (I can't because....)
- Blaming others (it's not my fault)
- Juggling too much (you will drop a ball)
- Saying "yes" to everything (even the wrong things)
- Playing it safe (fear of failure)
- Exhibiting arrogance (pride, ego)
- Avoiding change (refusing to adapt)
- Running over people to get what you want (valuing results over relationships)
- Trying to skip the first two steps on the Ladder of Influence (attempting to skip steps will cost you!)

As you read this, it may seem like a nearly impossible list of things to remember and implement as you go about your (most likely) very busy life. Don't worry about getting it all right instantly. Begin by focusing on the one thing that is your greatest weakness. Once you've made significant progress there, choose another and begin to work on it.

Influence doesn't come from being perfect. It comes from realizing you aren't perfect and working to get better.

Chapter Nineteen

THE FOURTH STEP: INFLUENCE BASED ON COMMITMENT TO DEVELOPING OTHERS

"You can't take someone to the top of the mountain if you don't know the way."

~ Ria Story

The first three steps on the Ladder of Influence are about becoming successful as an individual. Success is something you strive for personally and professionally. It's about making your own life better. There is absolutely nothing wrong with that. But, a small percentage of people have the courage to continue climbing. And, the way to keep climbing is to help others learn how to climb.

The fourth and fifth steps on the Ladder of Influence are about helping *others* become successful. At this step, we increase our influence because of what we are doing or have done to develop others, personally and/or professionally.

The amount of sacrifice required to climb past the third step prevents many people from attempting it. If we are going to help others, we must give up something: time, energy, money, etc. This requires a much deeper level of commitment. But, our reward is a greater amount of influence.

If you are working in a formal position of authority such as a business owner, CEO of a corporation, director, manager, supervisor, etc., then hopefully you realize part of your role as a leader is to develop those who are on your team. There are many resources available. You can find a list of recommendations in the Resources Appendix.

To be a highly effective "high impact" leader, you must help your team members and those in your organization develop their character and competency. Climbing the Ladder of Influence as a leader equips you to help others climb. During your climb, you gain valuable experience that will help you motivate and inspire others.

Keep this in mind. Even if you aren't in a formal position of authority, you can still help develop others and increase your influence with them at this level.

Helping others without a position of authority may mean you are mentoring someone younger than you. The great thing about this is, the older you get, the more people there are who are younger than you. You could teach a class or invest time with someone who looks up to you as a role model. You could help others using your social media platform. But, you won't have as much influence with your social media "friends" as you will with your real friends. Never overlook the value of developing real, face-to-face relationships.

Anyone who has climbed the Ladder of Influence and achieved success personally and professionally has an opportunity to give back to those who haven't. At this point, it's not about skill. It's about will.

Will you help? You must be humble enough to help, secure enough to help, and confident enough to help.

Many times, we may dream of helping many. But, we must be willing to start by helping just one. Brendon Burchard had this to say, *"Most people are not afraid to start their dream. They are embarrassed to be seen starting small."*

Having a *Commitment to Developing Others* isn't necessarily about speaking from a stage to thousands of people or writing a best-selling book. It's about being committed to developing others wherever you find them. The key is to help those who need help relative to your strengths, your passion, and your purpose. If you've mastered steps one through three, you will have the humility to start small with just one person.

To effectively help others, security and confidence in your character and competency is a must. In my book *"Leadership Gems: 30 Characteristics of Very Successful Leaders,"*

I wrote about the two basic types of confidence: self-confidence and situational-confidence.

Self-confidence is conviction of your values and core beliefs enhanced by experience and lessons learned from both successes and failures. In other words, self-confidence is static and is based on your character. The factors that make you uniquely you create your self-confidence. Self-confidence is developed over time. While other people can support you, self-confidence will only be realized by growing and developing your own character.

Situational-confidence is certainty of the outcome of a situation based on your talents, abilities, skills, and knowledge. In other words, situational-confidence is dynamic (it depends on the situation) and is affected by factors beyond your control. Situational-confidence can be increased by developing your competency.

You won't always have situational-confidence. There will be times when you try something new, take on a new job, or first become a manager and lack experience or technical knowledge. There will be times when you have a new relationship with a team member and lack confidence in their ability to get the job done.

You may have self-confidence because it's based on your character, which remains the same from one situation to the next, while lacking situational-confidence. For example, you may lack situational-confidence in a new job but still have plenty of self-confidence in your ability to learn the new job.

The previous example reveals strength of character because it takes self-confidence to put ourselves in a position to develop situational-confidence. To effectively develop others, you'll need a high degree of self-confidence and situational-confidence. Be confident but not cocky.

Chapter Twenty

CLIMBING TO THE
FOURTH STEP

"Always remember that who you're becoming is far more important than what you are doing, and yet it is what you're doing that is determining who you're becoming."

~ Hal Elrod

A *Commitment to Developing Others* is different than philanthropy. Philanthropy means "someone who loves humanity" and includes things like volunteering, giving money to a charity, or donating time and talent for a specific cause. Philanthropy isn't a bad thing at all – but a *Commitment to Developing Others* is a focused investment into the life and success of someone else. It's more purposeful and intentional than philanthropy, regardless of whether it's one person or many people.

Anyone can be a philanthropist no matter where they are on the Ladder of Influence.

Sometimes, you may have a heart to serve or to give back, but until you have truly climbed the Ladder of Influence and mastered the first three steps and beyond, you don't really have the foundation needed to become highly effective at developing others. And, that's okay.

What ultimately determines if someone wants to climb to the fourth step is if they continue growing after they have mastered the first three steps. Some people reach the third step and choose to stop there and enjoy their success, feeling as if they have achieved their mission in life. Even if they have no active desire to keep climbing at that point, if they continue developing their character, the natural result will be a desire to reach down and help others climb.

Note: You can't begin effectively climbing to the fourth step if you haven't yet mastered the first three steps. In other words, you can't help others master a level if you can't master it yourself. You can't raise the bar for others if you can't reach it yourself.

Five conditions must be met in order for you effectively develop others:

1) **You must value others.** Choosing to climb to the fourth step on the Ladder of Influence means you value others enough to help them become successful. And, you are willing to sacrifice for them because you value them.

   No one can make you sacrifice, so you will be able to help others. You must authentically value making sacrifices for others, and then, choose to do it. You can't fake it until you make it at step four.

   Although everyone has the potential to climb to the fourth step, not everyone will have the desire to do it.

2) **They must value growth.** You cannot force someone to grow because you cannot force them to make the necessary sacrifices nor can you develop discipline within them. They must be willing to give up in order to go up. Until they do, they're stuck.

3) **You must believe in others.** As you climb to the fourth step, you transition from producing results to helping others produce results. To make this transition, you must believe others have the ability to climb the Ladder of Influence just like you did. You must also be able to recognize a person's hidden potential. You must be able to see in them what they can't yet see in themselves.

4) **They must believe in themselves.** Often, you will believe in others more than they believe in themselves. When this happens, they can "borrow" your belief in them if they trust you. You must be able to help them

feel what you see. They will likely rise to the level of belief you express to them as they begin to believe in themselves with your support. However, you cannot develop those who aren't willing to believe in themselves. You can stretch them to some degree, based on what you believe they're capable of achieving. But if they don't truly develop a sincere belief in themselves, they won't be able to sustain the gain.

5) **They must trust you.** Developing others requires them to trust you because they can't see what you see. It's like asking someone who is only 5' tall to trust you when you tell them what's on the other side of a 6' wall. They cannot see what they need to see, and you're asking them to take action based on their level of trust in your ability to see what they can't. Actions that make sense at a higher level of development don't always make sense for those who aren't there yet. Trust is a must.

Climbing to the fourth step on the Ladder of Influence results in mutual benefit. Those you are developing win, and you do too. John C. Maxwell said it this way, "*It's impossible to help others without helping yourself.*" You will feel extremely fulfilled because you are truly stepping into your purpose on purpose for a purpose.

If you don't value others enough to invest in their development, even in some small way, then it's time for serious self-reflection. When you intentionally develop your character to a high level, you will automatically value others at a high level. The greatest satisfaction in life is helping others develop, grow, and climb the Ladder of Influence. Helping others always helps you.

Chapter Twenty-One

THE FOURTH STEP
AT HOME

"Yesterday I was clever, so I wanted to change the world. Today I am wise, so I am changing myself."

~ Rumi

A *Commitment to Developing Others* at home is really about investing in the success of those closest to you. This could mean your children or spouse, but it could also mean relationships with relatives, friends, and people in general.

Having a desire to empower others, so they won't have to depend on you, is a sign of growth and maturity. You are demonstrating personal security and confidence when you are willing to share your knowledge rather than hoard it. When you are willing to celebrate the success of others without fearing they will outgrow you or outshine you, you demonstrate true strength of character.

However, you shouldn't give advice or wisdom if it isn't wanted. This is more challenging at home than at work because you will likely have more emotions around your personal relationships than your professional relationships. If you give unsolicited advice, others will likely feel judged or criticized. You risk rupturing the relationship at worst or losing some influence at best.

So, what do you do? You continue developing yourself. You learn to influence others through your listening skills and your ability to ask the right questions.

The ability to deeply listen to others is a powerful tool when it comes to increasing your influence. It's a critical skill in strengthening relationships. Learning to fully listen without thinking about something else or without thinking about what you want to say is one of the most important skills you can develop if you want to take your influence to the next level and beyond.

Learn to listen to what *is* being said and what *isn't* being said. Learn to listen, with your eyes, to body language. Learn to squint with your eyes and ears as you listen for emotions and feelings between words.

When you know how to ask the right questions and how to listen to the answers, you will master the ability to increase your influence during conversations. Go slow to go fast. As Stephen R. Covey said best, *"Seek first to understand, then to be understood."*

Listening comes first because until others feel you understand them, they are not interested in your influence, advice, wisdom, perspective, or suggestions. Until others *feel* understood, they *think* you don't understand.

Learning to listen is particularly important in your personal relationships, especially at home, because relationships at home tug on your heart.

It's ironic that we often talk about developing our communication skills such as writing or speaking, but rarely, if ever, do we focus on the importance of developing our listening skills.

You'll know you are on the right track when you can say:

☐ I listen without thinking about something else. *(I focus on what the other person is saying, instead of something I want to say or something I'd rather be doing.)*

☐ I practice empathic listening. *(I listen to others and empathize with their perspective, even when I disagree.)*

☐ I listen without interrupting. *(I give the other person space to complete their sentence.)*

☐ I listen until the other person stops talking. *(I make sure others have finished sharing what's on their mind before I begin speaking.)*

☐ I give my full attention when listening. *(I don't look at my phone, computer, TV, etc. while listening.)*

☐ I show my attention with my body language. *(I stop what I'm doing, turn towards others, and focus on listening.)*

☐ I don't multitask when engaged in important conversations. *(I don't try to do other things while listening.)*

☐ I pay close attention to what isn't being said. *(I watch body language to learn more about what others are feeling.)*

☐ I reflect feelings when others are upset. *(I rephrase what I think they are saying and feeling to make sure they feel that I truly understand.)*

☐ I hold the space while others are thinking. *(I don't ask a question and then start talking if others don't reply immediately.)*

☐ I value my relationship with the other person more than I value winning the argument. *(It's not about being "right.")*

☐ I don't give unsolicited advice. *(I wait until I'm asked to give advice before telling others what I would do if I were them or what I think they should do in a particular situation.)*

Chapter Twenty-Two

THE FOURTH STEP
AT WORK

"Above all, a good teacher is one who continues to learn along with the students."

~ Carol Dweck

When you have a *Commitment to Developing Others* in a work environment, you realize the power of increasing your influence through asking questions. And of course, you make a habit of listening to the answers.

Climbing to the fourth step at work is about helping others develop themselves in an effort to motivate and inspire them to unleash their potential. At this step, you begin to realize it's not about you. But, you also understand it absolutely started with you. Your development has prepared you to develop others.

This is not about training or teaching someone how to perform a task at work. It's about helping others climb to the first, second, and third steps on the Ladder of Influence. You're reaching down, giving others a helping hand, and supporting them while they climb.

Avoid the temptation of trying to make others conform to your expectations. Influence at this step is gained when you're able to help others become successful on their terms *as defined by them*, not you. Two great ways to do this are: 1) Coaching (asking questions); and 2) Mentoring (sharing your perspective based on your experience).

If you're in a formal position of authority, learn how to coach your team members by asking questions. Mack offers great insight on leading with questions in his book, *"10 Values of High Impact Leaders."*

However, if you aren't in a formal leadership position, you can still climb to the fourth step at work by helping others become successful as you help them develop themselves – even if it means they get promoted or they leave for a better opportunity in a different organization.

Developing others means helping them develop the ability to think for themselves at a higher level. Asking questions is a great way to do this. To help others develop their own solutions, you must not be attached to their answers. Sometimes, you may not like their answers. Sometimes, you may disagree with their answers. That's okay. The goal is to facilitate *their* development. The goal isn't to manipulate them into doing what *you* would do.

Certainly, there are times when it's appropriate to share your insights and experience – but only with permission and only when you have developed a strong relationship. You will seldom increase your influence by simply telling someone what you think they should do. They will likely feel you are judging or criticizing them and/or their ideas. More importantly, they may not be bought into the solution – since it's not *their* solution.

If you feel they haven't arrived at the best solution, you should start asking better questions. But, don't start giving them directions and telling them what to do. The moment you begin to give unsolicited advice, you begin to force a solution and create distrust. Instead, keep asking questions until they develop a solution.

When helping others find their own solutions, I like to use a simple coaching model I created called PATH:

P: What is the **Purpose**?
- What is the purpose of our conversation?
- What problem are you trying to solve?
- What place are you trying to reach?
- What issue are you struggling with?
- What is the root cause of this issue?
- Why is this a challenge?

A: What is your current **Actuality**?

- How far are you away from where you want to be?
- What are the roadblocks you are facing?
- What is happening? Why?
- What is preventing you from taking action? Why?
- What does success look like for you?
- What kind of resources do you have right now?
- Who can help you?

T: What are the possible **Tracks** you can choose from?

- What else can you do?
- What would happen if you did this?
- What are the options on this path?
- What are the potential benefits?
- What are the possible negative outcomes?
- What would stop you?
- What can you do to make success more likely?
- Who else might this impact?
- What other choices do you have?
- If your life depended on action, what would you do?

H: Which **Highway** will you take?

- What's the best option?
- It's time to act – which course will you choose?
- What steps do you need to take right now? Next?
- What's your overall action plan?
- When will you complete it?
- Are you fully committed to this course of action? (If not, then find another Highway to travel!)

Chapter Twenty-Three

MASTERING THE
FOURTH STEP

"The high destiny of the individual is to serve rather than to rule."
~ Albert Einstein

You will know you are mastering the fourth step on the Ladder of Influence when you are: 1) Developing the right people at the right time in the right way for the right reasons; 2) Aligning yourself in the center of your lane 90% or more of the time; and 3) Saying "no" without hesitation to nearly everything outside of your lane.

As you master the fourth step, you will notice more people begin approaching you for mentorship and coaching. You will likely become more selective about who you help, how you help, and when you help.

Everyone has growth potential, but not everyone is interested or committed to growth. More specifically, not everyone is interested in sacrificing to grow. Many people like the thought of a mentor and coach, but not everyone has the humility, accountability, and commitment required to be mentored or coached.

Developing the right people is critical because you want to invest your time with people who are prepared to grow, willing to be stretched, and who will work hard to apply what they're learning.

I look for people who are prepared for our session – this demonstrates they are ready to grow. I look for people who are not afraid to try (and maybe fail) more than once – this reveals they are willing to be stretched. And, I look for people who will apply what they are learning.

If someone asks me for advice and I suggest a book as a helpful resource, I expect them to read it. If they don't read it, that reveals to me that they aren't willing to apply what they are learning. And, it proves to me they aren't yet fully invested in achieving their own success. That's okay. I don't blame them, but I also won't be investing much time with them. I want to help those who are committed to helping themselves.

As you master this fourth step, you will hone your ability to determine if the situation calls for coaching (asking questions) or mentoring (sharing experiences or insight). Both are highly valuable and developing others requires both skills as well as an ability to discern when to use one or the other. Many situations call for a blend of both skills. As a general rule: Listen first, then ask questions, and finally share your insights if the person is open to it and you have a great relationship with them.

Mastery of anything requires focused dedication and a *Commitment to Developing Others* is no exception. You cannot master this step if you are constantly choosing to step outside your lane. Make sure you are developing others within your area of expertise. Developing others is more like being a tour guide than a travel agent. You want to take people to a place you've been and are familiar with, not a place you've only heard about.

People who want to grow prefer to learn from someone who is higher up the Ladder of Influence than they are. You must know that you can't model a level of character you haven't reached yet. You must also know that you won't be a credible resource for others relative to competency if you don't actually know what they need to know. To be best positioned to help others develop their character and/or competency, you must be higher on the Ladder of Influence than they are.

For example, I wouldn't try to develop others in marketing or sales because it's not my field. I don't have competency strengths in those areas and wouldn't be of much help. Also, because it would require me to step out of my lane, it would not be a great use of my time. I would be doing them a disservice because they might be missing out on opportunities to learn from someone who does excel in those areas.

My focus is on developing others in my lane of influence: Personal Success and Leadership Development.

There will always be someone above us on the Ladder of Influence. Don't focus on those people. You shouldn't be trying to help those people. They are ahead of you. You should be helping those who are still striving to climb to the levels you have mastered. There are plenty of people in the world who need your help. Focus on developing them.

You must become an expert at saying "no" to the opportunities that fall outside your lane. You cannot help everyone nor can you do everything for everybody. You will increase your influence at a much greater pace if you focus on staying in the center of your lane where you're best positioned to do the most good for the most people. If you choose to step into another lane, you won't be in your lane when someone shows up needing your help.

This concept is difficult for many because if they have mastered the fourth step and have a *Commitment to Developing Others*, it's because they truly want to help others. Saying "no" to others when you have a heart to help may be hard for you. But remember, saying "no" to people outside your lane gives you the freedom to say "yes" to the people in your lane.

I like the analogy of juggling to help you see this principle. Most of us can "juggle" one rubber ball (lane). If we only have one ball, we will easily be able to toss it from one hand to the other without losing focus. But, every time we attempt to add another ball (lane), our focus becomes diminished. One is easy. Five is not.

You may not choose to narrow your focus and stay in your lane. But remember, you will be less effective. As a result, you won't build as much trust and influence.

Chapter Twenty-Four

FIFTH STEP:
INFLUENCE BASED ON
CONTRIBUTION OF
SERVICE OVER TIME

"Leader is not a title that the world gives to you – it's an offering that you give the world."

~ Abby Wambach

When it comes down to it, we choose whether we want to climb the Ladder of Influence or not. Everyone has some influence (either positive or negative), but not everyone will choose to increase their positive influence by intentionally climbing from step to step.

Success is about achieving what we want in life. It's about earning what we want for ourselves. When we achieve success, we have learned to effectively climb *our* ladder. We decide what success means to us.

There is absolutely nothing wrong with that.

But, something greater is possible.

Some who achieve success will feel the call to move beyond success for themselves and truly become significant in the lives of others. Some who have climbed their own ladder won't be fulfilled until they go back down and start helping others climb their ladder.

Some will choose to do this for a few others as they work on the fourth step, *Commitment to Developing Others.* However, some will master the fourth step and then contribute a lifetime of service helping others climb.

This is how a legacy is created.

Legacy is about continuously making a difference in the lives of others year after year. Legacy requires you to sacrifice endlessly for the rest of your life.

This is what self-realization is all about.

Becoming the best version of yourself means you *become* who you were created to *be* and fulfill the mission you were created to accomplish. When you do this for an extended period of your life, you will build influence based on your *Contribution of Service Over Time.*

Your legacy is a testament of how you have lived and what you have done to help others. When you make it to the fifth step, others have begun to respect you for who you are, the work you have done, how you have done it, and how many you have helped throughout your life. At this level, your influence extends far beyond those you know. You will influence people you've never met. You will continue influencing others after your death.

When we think of people throughout history around the world who have reached the fifth step on the Ladder of Influence, they all have three things in common: 1) They all led themselves well; 2) They all mastered the first four steps on the Ladder of Influence; and 3) They all had a cause greater than themselves.

Mother Teresa, Nelson Mandela, Martin Luther King Jr., are a few who immediately come to mind when I think of fifth step legacy influencers.

Maslow's *Hierarchy of Needs* begins at the bottom with basic needs (food, water, and shelter) and progresses up the levels to the top (self-actualization). Until the level below has been satisfied, it isn't possible to move up to the next level. You must start at the bottom and climb your way to the top.

In other words, it's rather difficult, or perhaps impossible, to reach your potential if you are scrambling each day to find food and a place to sleep. It's simply a matter of not being able to direct any energy toward fulfilling your calling because you must direct all of your energy toward fulfilling your basic needs. Although energy is never lost, time certainly is. Keep in mind, your energy *is* finite just like your time on earth.

Since you're reading this, you aren't likely scrambling to find food and shelter. But when we are unable to execute on the small daily disciplines, we will also be unable to fulfill the higher calling on our lives.

That's why *Control of Self* is the first step relative to influencing others. When you lead yourself well, you earn the right to influence others. Anyone who has ever reached the fifth step on the Ladder of Influence did so because they first learned to control themselves and their emotions.

Those who have influence based on their *Contribution of Service Over Time* will influence others long after they're gone. They will inspire others to strive for more, to be more, and to do more. Many will refer to them as "leaders" even if they never held a formal position of authority. As John C. Maxwell stated, *"Leadership is influence. Nothing more. Nothing less."*

We can refer to those who reach the fifth step on the Ladder of Influence as *leaders* or *influencers*. They are both. Regardless of the word we choose, we know their cause led them to lead and influence others. That cause is (or was) always greater than themselves.

This is an important point because certainly there are many people who have influenced thousands of people all over the world. Unfortunately, some of them chose to do it in very negative ways or for very selfish reasons. I'm sure you can think of a few people who developed tremendous negative influence with others.

Today, the term "influencer" often means someone who is using social media to influence many people quickly, usually for money. Certainly, that's one type of influence and one way to use it. But, you're not likely to establish a lasting *Contribution of Service Over Time* through social media.

Although climbing speeds may vary, there are no shortcuts on the Ladder of Influence. You must do the work within yourself in order to truly climb. You will never be able to reach the fifth step if you aren't willing to start at the bottom and relentlessly work your way to the top.

Chapter Twenty-Five

CLIMBING TO THE
FIFTH STEP

"The measure of your life will not be in what you accumulate, but in what you give away."

~ Wayne Dyer

Climbing to the fifth step on the Ladder of Influence is really a question of sacrifice. You can't simply decide to climb to the fifth step. You must make the choice to continuously sacrifice for others; and if you do this enough, for enough people, for long enough, society will determine when or if you reach and master the fifth step.

Certainly, some sacrifice was required for you to climb to the fourth step. However, a much greater sacrifice will be required to climb to the fifth step. There's no way to understand ahead of time exactly what type of sacrifice(s) you must make and how many.

Only you know the price you are willing to pay in order to keep climbing. What are you willing to sacrifice for your cause? Are you willing to sacrifice for your cause even if it's not appreciated until much later, perhaps not even until after your death? As Lieutenant General George Flynn U.S. Marine Corps stated, *"The cost of leadership (influence) is self-interest."*

Remember, your sacrifice may affect other people. You may be willing to sacrifice in order to climb to the fifth step, but don't forget that your spouse or children may not have the same perspective. How will your sacrifice affect them? Is that acceptable to you? To them?

How high will you climb? Climbing the Ladder of Influence is similar to climbing a mountain. Anyone who has climbed to the top of Mount Everest can tell you that it took countless hours preparation, work (before reaching the mountain), and extreme effort to climb to the top. But, it only takes one mistake to fall from the top.

The Ladder of Influence is the same in the sense that

climbing to the top is going to take countless hours of work, untold hours of development, extreme effort, and high energy. But, it may take only one mistake or small mishap, relative to your character, to cause you to fall. You can fall from any step on the Ladder of Influence. However, the higher you have climbed, the farther you have to fall, and the more public your fall will be.

Once you have reached the fourth step, there are three things that will help you climb to the fifth step on the Ladder of Influence. These three things will not only help you climb. They will also help keep you centered, so you are less likely to fall:

1) **Maintain Integrity.** With any gift or talent, there also comes a responsibility to use it well. The high level of influence and trust you build as you climb the Ladder of Influence is no different. As Stephen R. Covey reminds us, *"To touch the soul of another human being is to walk on holy ground."* Use your influence ethically. The minute you act without integrity or the minute you try to manipulate, use, or abuse someone with your influence is the moment you begin to slip off the Ladder of Influence. You may not realize it instantly, but it happens instantly. Sooner or later, your character is revealed. Choices always come with consequences, and the consequences of manipulating people will eventually catch up to you, one way or another. With a high degree of influence comes a certain measure of power. With power comes the possibility for corruption. Never forget, you can't skip steps on the Ladder of Influence and constant attention to your character is always required. Remember to examine your motives and maintain your integrity by staying true to your values.

2) **Maintain Humility.** Nothing, except a lack of integrity, will cause you to fall off the Ladder of Influence faster than arrogance. A certain degree of humility is required to help you maintain your integrity. Angola Prison Warden (former) Burl Cain said it best, *"You've got to be humble, so you don't stumble."* The essence of a high level of authentic influence is servant leadership, that is, a dedication to the service of others. That's what *Contribution of Service Over Time* is all about. It takes years, perhaps decades, to climb to the fifth step on the Ladder of Influence. You can't get there without humility, and you certainly won't remain there without humility. If serving others is beneath you, the fifth step will remain above you.

3) **Maintain Focus.** The fifth step on the Ladder of Influence is about living a purpose driven life and having purpose driven influence. This requires intentionality on a consistent, relentless, and daily basis. Establishing influence at this level has more to do with who you are than what you know and what you do. *Who* you are determines *what* you do, *why* you do it, and *who* you do it for or with. One of the greatest challenges you will face as time passes is remaining committed, consistent, and focused. Robert Rabbin suggested, *"Keep one degree of focus while maintaining 360 degrees of awareness. It means that we pay total attention to what is right in front of us, without losing awareness of all that is around us."*

Passion creates focus.
Purpose maintains focus.

Chapter Twenty-Six

THE FIFTH STEP
AT HOME

"Few things are as encouraging as the realization that things can be different and that we have a role in making them so."

~ Daniel Taylor

As you climb to the fifth step, you should realize the public in general will form an opinion of you based on what they know about you. The reality is that if you aren't careful, your public profile may not be an accurate reflection of who you are all the time. And, the people who are closest to you at home will know it.

To some extent, this happens regardless of which step you are on. It's simply magnified to a much greater degree on the fifth step.

Most people act certain ways with certain people in certain social settings and act in different ways with different people in different social settings. As we grow and develop our character, our various personas should start blending together until we are one authentic person, no matter where we are or who we're with.

If you have a high degree of character, you are happy to reveal it everywhere with everyone. But, if you have a low degree of character, you likely attempt to conceal it in some places with some people. You can mask your character, but you'll never be able to hide it.

Your character and characteristics should be the same on Friday night out with your friends as they are on Sunday morning in church or Monday morning at work. In other words, as you grow and develop your character, you should be conscious of being authentic in every situation. If you are "walking the talk," you should be walking it at home, at work, at sporting events, in traffic, everywhere you go.

A poor example would be someone who pretends to be a proactive, self-controlled person in public who regularly loses control at home with their family members.

Or, a manager who treats their team poorly but pretends to care about them when talking with others.

As Mack says, *"Who we are some of the time is who we are all of the time."* In other words, who we are in our worst moments is a true reflection of our character.

A good indication of your growth and authenticity is the moment you realize you no longer feel the need to hide your behavior. Not because you are always perfect, but because you own your behavior and are working to improve it. Your influence doesn't come from being perfect because everyone around you already knows you aren't. They just aren't always sure YOU know it, or if you care. The moment you own your character weaknesses is the moment you begin to overcome them.

Many public figures have had very public downfalls when their true character was revealed – and it wasn't the same level of character they *claimed* to have. Generally, the people who are closest to you, at home, see the side of you that the public doesn't get to see. They know the truth. Make sure they see the same "you" that everyone else sees. Strive to be one person. As Ralph Waldo Emerson stated, *"Who you are speaks so loudly I cannot hear what you say."*

You will know you are on track when you can say:

- ☐ I apologize immediately when I wrong someone. *(I don't wait to fix my wrongs.)*

- ☐ I accept feedback on my character weaknesses from those closest to me. *(I am working to get better and will take all the help I can get.)*

- ☐ I treat others with kindness at all times. *(I don't pretend to be kind, and then, act rudely to a server or someone I don't know.)*

☐ I use the same language at home, at work, at a party, with close friends, and with extended family. *(I don't use profanity with some while pretending I don't speak that way with others.)*

☐ It would be okay if everyone knew what I read, watch, or listen to. *(I'm transparent about my values and what I allow to influence my mind.)*

☐ I speak truthfully. *(I don't try to deceive anyone.)*

☐ I'll share any of my jokes with anyone: spouse, family, friends, boss, co-workers, at church, etc. *(I know the jokes I tell or laugh at reveal a lot about my true character.)*

☐ I don't feel the need to hide certain things from certain people. *(I don't attempt to hide any of my behaviors and habits from anyone.)*

☐ I make sure my social media content accurately portrays me. *(I don't have a reason to mask my character. I'm okay with revealing the real me to others.)*

☐ I don't criticize others for behaviors I practice. *(I am not two-faced. If I behave in certain ways publicly, privately, or secretly, I don't criticize others who exhibit the same behaviors.)*

☐ I don't have to worry if my friends, family, co-workers, or clients talk to each other. *(I'm consistently the same person with everyone.)*

Chapter Twenty-Seven

THE FIFTH STEP
AT WORK

"The goal in life is not to live forever. The goal in life is to create something that does."

~ John C. Maxwell

A sign of someone who is truly climbing to the fifth step on the Ladder of Influence at work is that they focus less on being needed and focus more on being succeeded. In other words, you focus more on developing others to grow beyond you and not to be dependent on you.

Once you have climbed to the fifth step, you will have a "platform." How you use your platform will determine your legacy. A lasting legacy means something is carried forward, and it doesn't end in your absence. Who you are and what you've done will impact others long after your death. Your influence doesn't die with you. It lives on.

Your legacy is what you leave *in* others rather than what you leave *for* others. It's not about leaving others money or material things, it's about leaving others better than they were before you begin to influence them. Perhaps the greatest legacy you can leave is to motivate and inspire your followers to leave their own legacy.

If you weren't here tomorrow, who would fill your shoes? More importantly, are they going to temporarily attempt to fill your shoes, actually fill your shoes, or have you prepared them to eventually outgrow your shoes?

Many times great influencers mentor others and develop them, but they are developing people to follow in their footsteps rather than to forge their own path. There is nothing wrong with this as long as everyone is clear about what's really happening and shares the same goal. Are you equipping others with the knowledge, skills, and mentorship to carry on *your* legacy or to create *their own*?

I believe a high impact leader can only establish a track record of *Contribution of Service Over Time* if they have a high degree of humility that allows them to realize sooner rather than later – Their legacy began with them, but it's not about them.

Mother Teresa didn't simply work in the slums of India. She intentionally developed others, so they could carry on long after she was gone, even in places where she had never been. It started with her, but it wasn't about her.

You don't need to be (or have been) world famous to reach the *Contribution of Service Over Time* step on the Ladder of Influence. A teacher who touches the lives of students during years of dedicated service can climb to this level of influence by first impacting the lives of students, then by impacting their children through them. The teacher may never teach their student's children. However, if the teacher made a lasting impact on the students, the students changed, their lives changed, and eventually those changes impacted the lives of their children.

Climbing to the fifth step on the Ladder of Influence isn't about being world-famous. It's about making an impact in the lives of others, right where you are, in the work you are called to do. Your goal should be to develop others who will do the same in their own way.

Remember, you can't simply decide to climb to the fifth step. You must decide to dedicate your life to serving where you are led to serve, make the sacrifices to do so at a high level, and focus on living out of your purpose. Those whom you serve will be the ones who decide if and when you truly reach the fifth step. You'll know you are traveling on the right path when you can confidently say:

☐ I am regularly mentoring several people to help them identify where they can make their own *Contribution of Service. (I am helping them create their own legacy, even if it means they aren't continuing in mine.)*

☐ I know exactly what work I am called to do, and I'm doing it almost exclusively. *(I focus on fulfilling my purpose more than 90% of the time.)*

☐ I realize my purpose is not about me, but it starts with me. *(I know the work I'm doing is more important than who I am, where I came from, or where I end up.)*

☐ I am more concerned with the impact I'm making than the sacrifices I've made. *(What I'm working for is more important to me than what I had to give up to do it.)*

☐ I am continuing to develop my competency and skills. *(I realize growth is a journey that never ends.)*

☐ I am continuing to develop my leadership skills. *(I have a responsibility as a leader of others, and I'm making sure I master that responsibility.)*

☐ There are many people following me and the work I do. *(I am building a tribe of followers who are willing to allow me to help them create their own legacy.)*

☐ I have determined how my contribution will remain relevant after I am gone. *(I've created content that will outlive me. I have helped develop others to succeed me. I know there are others who will continue or even expand the cause.)*

☐ People I have never met know who I am and the impact I am making or have made. *(I have a reputation of respect based on my Contribution of Service Over Time.)*

Chapter Twenty-Eight

MASTERING THE FIFTH STEP

"Many are known for what they have taken. I would rather be known for what I have given."

~ Beswick Barrington

Mastering the fifth step isn't really about getting anywhere or climbing any higher. It's about becoming more and more of who you were meant to be. Because at some point, the purpose of your growth isn't to take you anywhere different than where you are but rather for you to become the best you can be right where you are.

Contribution of Service Over Time is about the lasting legacy you create by living one intentional day followed by another, one intentional choice at a time, one intentional encounter at a time…compounded over a lifetime.

It will take years of relentless dedication to master the fifth step. At this step, it's about your cumulative impact. Your influence at this step is based on the collective positive impact you have made in all of the lives you have touched along your journey.

Mastering the fifth step requires you to first master yourself. It means you have the ability, have taken responsibility, and have the willingness to focus on improving yourself first before shifting your focus to helping others climb.

Influence at this step is very much developed as you lead by example and model what you've learned because your followers (and many others) will always be watching.

Saying one thing but doing another will destroy your credibility and influence, especially at the fifth step. Once your credibility has been wrecked, it may be rebuilt. But, it will never be the same.

Be careful. Be intentional. Then, be resilient.

It's what you do with what you've been given that counts. None of us were born into the same circumstances, had the same experiences, or traveled the same path. A lack of opportunity or a life of adversity doesn't disqualify you from reaching the fifth step on the Ladder of Influence. In fact, it may give you strength.

Consider the following examples:

Victor Frankl was imprisoned in concentration camps by the Nazis. He lost his family and his wife but went on to write one of the most influential books ever written.

Franklin Roosevelt was paralyzed by polio and went on to serve as the President of the United States.

Oprah Winfrey was born into poverty to a single mother in Mississippi and faced abuse in her early years and went on to host the highest rated TV show (of its kind) in history.

Nick Vujicic was born with no arms and no legs. Today, he is one of the world's top motivational speakers.

Malala Yousafzai was shot in the head by the Taliban when she was 15 for advocating for education for girls. But, she survived and later won the Nobel Peace Prize.

The list of people who have made a dramatic impact after experiencing extreme adversity seems endless. If you become discouraged, do an internet search for "people who have overcome adversity." You'll likely develop a different perspective about your own circumstances. We can always find someone who has it worse than we do.

My great-grandmother "Granny Beverett" used to tell me, *"Thank God it's as good as it is."*

Wise words indeed.

Influencers come from around the world and throughout history. Each has faced their own unique adversity. We all have. It's part of the human condition.

We all have chapters in our stories that are tough, painful, even heartbreaking at times. But, what happens to us is not as important as who we become because of it.

As Bob Goff says, *"Things that go wrong can shape us or scar us."* Many times, adversity in our lives becomes the seed from which our *Contribution of Service* sprouts.

Honor where you are as you move to where you want to be.

You should strive to be remembered as a person with a high degree of character who treated small and large responsibilities the same. At the fifth step, there are no small responsibilities because they all have a large impact.

Les Brown said, *"When you decide to pursue greatness, you are taking responsibility for your life. This means you are choosing to accept the consequences of your actions, and to become the agent of your mental, physical, spiritual, and material success. You may not always be able to control what life puts in your path, but I believe you can always control who you are."*

Becoming the best version of you, whatever that looks like, will require personal transformation. It won't happen by accident. You must transform from who you are today into who you have the potential to become.

Transformation doesn't happen in one day. It happens every day. You won't be able to look at yourself after one day of growth and see much, if any, difference. But, if you look at yourself after 365 days of intentional daily growth or 1,825 days (5 years), you will be shocked by how far you can go when you become intentional about growth.

Everyone who got to where they are started from where they were. Only YOU can hold you back. Only YOU can define what success at the fifth step means for you. Only YOU can make the choices that will help you master the fifth step. YOU determine what YOU will and won't do.

At the fifth step, you know it started with you, but you also know it won't end with you.

Chapter Twenty-Nine

MOUNTAIN MOMENTS

"Those who change the world start by changing themselves."

~ Ria Story

Great lives are made up of great years. Great years are made up of great days. Great days are made up of great hours. Great hours are made up of great minutes. And, great minutes are made up of great moments.

Every moment isn't always a great moment, but every moment can become a defining moment. Every moment brings possibility and the potential to take us closer to or farther away from our destination. **It's the choices we make that determine if a moment is great or not.** Every choice we make determines who we are *becoming.*

Don't worry about getting every choice right for the rest of your life. Focus on getting the next choice right. If you simply do that over and over again, the rest of your life will take care of itself.

It may feel like you're climbing a mountain. A really big mountain. Think Mount Everest.

My husband Mack Story says, *"When you are climbing a mountain, don't focus on the mountain ahead. Focus on the moment at hand. Conquer each moment, and you will conquer the mountain."*

But, you must keep climbing.

My friend and author Allison Michels said this, *"Small victories every day lead to greatness. Now, go climb your own mountain and always remember to KEEP GOING!"*

Climbing the Ladder of Influence is also similar to driving through a heavy fog. The headlights of your car won't shine far into a heavy fog, so you can't see much of what's ahead of you. But one thing is certain. If you don't move forward, you will simply remain stuck in the fog. You must keep moving to make it out of the fog.

When it comes to climbing your Ladder of Influence, you aren't always going to be able to see where it will take you. In fact, you can't begin to imagine all the possibilities that will open up as you climb higher.

Your growth-oriented goal is simple: keep climbing.

By now, you should realize there is no destination. You're on an endless journey. You never stop climbing. Although you may reach the fifth and final step, you're still working to strengthen every step on *your* ladder. You never get to forget about the lower steps. *Control of Self* and *Character Development* are the greatest challenges for us all. The higher you climb, the more important it becomes not to forget about the importance of those first two steps.

When you reach the fourth and fifth steps on the Ladder of Influence, you will have a much greater level of influence and therefore a much greater level of responsibility. The higher you climb, the greater your impact. When you fall off the first step, only a few people will be impacted. When you fall off the top step, a lot of people will be impacted.

The most difficult person in the world for you to influence is the one that's always looking back at you when you step in front of a mirror. It's not the lack of knowledge that holds us back. It's failing to apply what we know.

Inevitably, you will fail. It's part of being human. We all have flaws. Part of the human experience is making mistakes. When you have developed a high degree of character, each of your failures feel huge because the higher you climb, the more you value maintaining your integrity.

Reflect and learn from those moments.

You won't ever stop having challenges in life. But, they will appear smaller in hindsight if you continue to grow and learn from them. The greater you become, the greater the size of the obstacles and challenges you will be able to overcome. Keep going and keep growing.

Think back to when you were a teenager. Didn't your

problems seem ENORMOUS? Yet today when you look back, you realize most, if not all, of them weren't as big as they appeared at the time. That's not because the problem or challenge got smaller. It's because you've grown. As a result, you're better equipped to deal with adversity.

The problems and challenges you face today and tomorrow present the same opportunity. Obstacles always look bigger when you're closest to them. But, once you overcome them and put some distance between them and you, they begin to appear smaller and smaller. If you learn from them and grow through them, you will be able to benefit in the future when new challenges appear.

At times when making tough choices, you will feel as if you're fighting the gravitational pull of Jupiter, which is approximately two and a half times greater than Earth's gravity according to worldatlas.com. Other times, you will feel in the moment like some choices don't matter at all, especially if they seem like "small" choices.

Don't forget. Small choices will compound over time. Small wins add up over time. Small losses do too. Small everyday choices in the wrong direction can slow you down. Small choices can discourage you and may derail you completely. Traveling in the wrong direction will only delay your journey.

You don't have to win every battle to win the war. But, you will never win the battles you don't fight. Focus on winning each moment and leading yourself well no matter the situation. Every time you are successful, you will create momentum that will help you climb a little easier, a little faster, and a little farther. Every time you struggle, you will slow a bit and feel the climb getting a little steeper.

As we climb the Ladder of Influence, the choices we make each day will push us higher or pull us lower.

Chapter Thirty

KEEP CLIMBING

"The biggest adventure you can ever take is to live the life of your dreams."

~ Oprah Winfrey

Once you become familiar with the steps on the Ladder of Influence, you will start to see everything from a different perspective.

Often, when we aren't able to influence others, we tend to blame them. That's natural. As I shared in chapter one, we blame others because it's easy. As long as it's "their fault," then we don't have to do anything to correct, change, or improve the situation. When we shoulder the responsibility for increasing our influence, we are taking on the responsibility for leading ourselves well in an effort to increase our positive influence with others who share our values.

The moment you begin blaming others, you begin to destroy trust and lose influence.

Guard against the temptation to judge others. As you climb higher on the Ladder of Influence, it will be easier for you to determine where others are relative to their climb. Their climb will be different than yours. Remember, you can't control anyone. You can't make them climb faster. All you can do is focus on controlling yourself in a way that increases your influence with others.

Your climb will always be uphill.

You can't "unlearn" something once you have learned it. It's much like learning how to read. If you recognize words you're familiar with, you can't see them without knowing what they mean. Now that you have a better understanding of the consequences of everything you think, say, and do, you can't help but realize how much it matters.

There will be times when you don't want to climb.

You will get tired of feeling the pressure (from within) to do the right things all the time. Your inner two-year-old self is going to want to cave to the emotions of the moment, quit, or do the easy thing instead of the right thing. This is more likely to happen when you're tired, stressed, hurt, or emotionally drained.

Don't do it. Don't give in. Don't quit. Don't give up.

You must keep going, keep growing, and keep climbing. Stay the course. You're on the right track.

Something inside you is dreaming of how you can make your corner of the world a better place. Your definition of "better" is going to be different from everyone else's. That's okay. Your purpose is unique to you, and only you can fulfill it.

As long as we are alive and have hope, we're always dreaming of how life can be better. We all crave purpose and meaning in our lives. We all crave more influence with the people around us and those we want to help.

Certainly, life will be better if we increase our influence. The more positive influence we have with those around us, the easier it becomes to be successful in any endeavor.

The greatest heartbreak stems from the dreams that weren't fulfilled, the legacies that weren't fulfilled, the books that weren't written, the stories that weren't told, the ideas that weren't implemented, the businesses that weren't started, or the potential that wasn't realized because someone was too afraid to act or wasn't committed to making it happen.

One of the quotes that has always inspired me is Theodore Roosevelt's "*Man in the Arena,*" which was part of a speech he delivered in 1910, more than 100 years ago:

"It is not the critic who counts; not the man who points out how

the strong man stumbles, or where the doer of deeds could have done them better. The credit belongs to the man who is actually in the arena, whose face is marred by dust and sweat and blood; who strives valiantly; who errs, who comes up short again and again, because there is no effort without error and shortcoming; but who does actually strive to do the deeds; who knows great enthusiasms, the great devotions; who spends himself in a worthy cause; who at the best knows in the end the triumph of high achievement, and who at the worst, if he fails, at least fails while daring greatly, so that his place shall never be with those cold and timid souls who neither know victory nor defeat."

It reminds us that when we strive, we will sometimes fall short. When we "spend" for a worthy cause, we will know both triumph and failure. But, at least we will be able to claim we made the effort.

That's what life is about.

Because without striving to become the best person we are capable of becoming, life becomes meaningless. Empty. Dull. Pointless. And, when life is empty, we will try to fill the void with empty things. But, they won't bring any lasting satisfaction, and we will be left unfulfilled and dissatisfied.

Living life to the fullest isn't about having the most things, the most money, the biggest house, or the most social media followers. Living life to the fullest is about stepping into your potential. It's about maximizing not only your potential, but your results, both personally and professionally. Don't settle for a life unlived.

Your dreams are inside you because you are capable of making them come true. But, only you can do it.

The greatest discovery you will ever make is realizing you hold the key to success in life. The most difficult challenge you will ever undertake is to lead and influence *yourself* in a way that allows you to realize it. Keep climbing!

RESOURCES APPENDIX

Download free chapters from most of Ria and Mack's books at:
RiaStory.com/Download

PERSONAL DEVELOPMENT

1) Fearfully and Wonderfully Me: Become the Woman You are Destined to Be, Ria Story
2) PRIME Time: The Power of Effective Planning, Ria Story
3) 10 Foundational Elements of Intentional Transformation, Mack Story
4) Blue-Collar Leadership®: Leading from the Front Lines, Mack Story
5) Defining Influence, Mack Story
6) The 7 Habits of Highly Effective People, Stephen R. Covey
7) The Five Levels of Attachment, Don Miguel Ruiz, Jr.
8) The 5 Love Languages, Dr. Gary Chapman
9) Leadership and Self-Deception, Arbinger Institute

PROFESSIONAL DEVELOPMENT

1) Straight Talk: The Power of Effective Communication, Ria Story
2) Change Happens: Leading Yourself and Others through Change, Mack and Ria Story
3) Creative Followership, Jimmy Collins
4) The Speed of Trust, Stephen M. R. Covey
5) Who's Buying You?, Mack Story
6) Blue-Collar Leadership® & Teamwork, Mack Story

IDENTIFYING YOUR PASSION/PURPOSE

1) ACHIEVE: Maximize Your Potential with 7 Keys to Unlock Success and Significance, Ria Story
2) Put Your Dream to the Test, John C. Maxwell
3) The Purpose Driven Life, Rick Warren
4) Start with Why, Simon Sinek
5) The 8th Habit, Stephen R. Covey

LEADERSHIP DEVELOPMENT

1) Leadership Gems/Leadership Gems for Women, Ria Story
2) Blue-Collar Leadership® & Culture: The 5 Components for Building High Performance Teams, Mack Story
3) Blue-Collar Leadership® & Supervision: Unleash Your Team's Potential, Mack Story
4) 10 Values of High Impact Leaders, Mack Story
5) The 5 Levels of Leadership, John C. Maxwell
6) Leaders Eat Last, Simon Sinek
7) The 21 Irrefutable Laws of Leadership, John C. Maxwell
8) It's Your Ship, Captain Michael Abrashoff

RESOURCES FOR PERSONAL GROWTH AND LEADERSHIP DEVELOPMENT

Access free preview chapters from Ria's other books at: RiaStory.com/Download

Find information on Ria's podcast at: RiaStory.com/Podcast

Watch Ria's TEDx talk: RiaStory.com/TEDx

Connect with Ria on Social:

Facebook: facebook.com/ria.story

Twitter: twitter.com/Ria_Story

LinkedIn: linkedin.com/in/riastory

Instagram: instagram.com/ria.story

**Or email Ria at:
Ria@RiaStory.com**

Excerpt from *Ria's Story From Ashes To Beauty,* by **Ria Story**

I was 12 when Dad started having some conversations with me about the *"facts of life."* He would tell me how infidelity in marriage was wrong and so was divorce. But, *"his needs"* weren't being met because my mother wasn't able to meet them. I was told they didn't have a physical relationship for many years, but I don't know if that is true. I know she was sleeping on the couch in the living room most nights, she said because of her back. I suspect I will never know the truth. I want to believe she had no idea what was going on, but it's possible she knew and didn't want to face reality, so she shut it out. Either version is hard for me to accept, but there are many things in life we don't want to accept.

I remember times when Mom was gone, out running errands or something, and my Dad would tell her to take my brother with her. At first, all our talks were about how I needed to be *"pure"* and stay away from boys until my Dad was able to find the *"Right one that God would send."* Then, it changed to being all about how a woman was designed by God to meet a man's needs and that was all I was created for. I remember feeling ashamed talking about things like that, but I didn't know what to do. It was the summer when I was 12 that he first started saying how a father-daughter relationship was supposed to be close in every way, physically as well as emotionally. I remember being told I was supposed to give my heart to him *"for safekeeping,"* but I was confused as to why that also meant in a physical way.

One day my Mom and brother were gone, and Dad and I were sitting in the living room *"talking."* Somehow, things turned into how wonderful it was that I was the perfect daughter and was so close to my Dad. We went upstairs, and he kept telling me how God intended for daughters to belong to daddies. And, if I would trust him, he would make sure I lived up to what God wanted. He told me how I was supposed to fill in since my Mother wasn't able to be a wife anymore. He told me I was living up to God's purpose for my life by helping him not have to commit adultery. He told me it wasn't a sin if I helped him like that. He took off my clothes and told me the whole time I was the perfect daughter.

What started out as just taking off my clothes progressed. Within a few months, it wasn't just taking off my shirt and jeans but taking off everything.

Deep in the back of a forgotten drawer, my Mom had hidden a bunch of lingerie she used to wear when she was young, and they were newly married. Dad brought it out one day while we were alone in the house together. He picked out one of the outfits and told me to go in the bathroom. Then, he wanted me to put it on and come out to model it for him. I cried afterward, ashamed of being looked at like that. I was sad for my Mom too – her personal things should not have been shared with anyone, much less her daughter.

Then, the touching started.

ORDER *RIA'S STORY FROM ASHES TO BEAUTY* ONLINE AT: AMAZON.COM OR RIASTORY.COM

Excerpt from *Straight Talk: The Power of Effective Communication,* by Ria Story

I was nearly 20 years old before I realized I liked people. I never considered myself to be an "introvert" although most people would have. I simply didn't talk to people. Ask me a question, and you would get a monosyllabic response that discouraged any further dialogue. It's not that I didn't want to talk or communicate with people – I simply didn't know how.

I grew up very isolated, living on a farm in the middle of the woods. I was homeschooled. We didn't attend church regularly, and my social contact growing up was mainly limited to field trips with other homeschoolers. In the early 1980's in Alabama, opportunities for homeschooled children to participate in extra-curricular activities were limited, and my parents didn't pursue most of them.

I was also sexually abused by my father from age 12 – 19. Growing up with feelings of shame, guilt, hurt, and unworthiness only compounded my natural tendency to be withdrawn, even after I left home at 19. I share more about my story in some of my other books, *Ria's Story From Ashes To Beauty* and *Beyond Bound and Broken: A Journey of Healing and Resilience.*

Leaving home without a job, a car, or even a high school diploma, I got a crash course on the need for communication in "normal" society.

At 19, I had a great education, ability to think critically, reasoning skills, proactive attitude, and willingness to work hard. What I didn't have was the critical ability to connect with other people and communicate *effectively.*

Since I didn't have a GED or a high school diploma,

finding a way to make a living wasn't going to be easy, but I was determined to start making money and earning my way.

My first job was working as a server at a pizza restaurant. I worked the lunch shift, Monday through Friday every day, from 11:00 – 2:00. Most customers would have the all-you-can-eat pizza and salad buffet because it was fast and didn't cost too much.

I was the only lunch server for all 36 tables in the restaurant. My job was to set up the buffet, keep the salad bar stocked and clean, make the tea, fill the ice bin, stock the soda machine, answer the phone, take delivery orders, greet the customers when they entered, take and fill their drink orders, keep dirty plates bussed, refill their drinks, check them out at the cash register, clean the tables, chairs, and floor after the customer left, wash all the dishes, put them away, and restock everything before I left. All for $2.13 per hour, plus any tips I made.

The lunch buffet was $5.99, and a drink was $1.35. Most customer bills came to less than $8.00 for lunch. The average tip is 10% for a buffet, so the best tip I could expect would be about $1.00 – and that's if I hustled really hard to keep their soda refilled and the dirty plates bussed. If I was too busy and the customer ran out of tea, I may not have gotten a tip at all.

I learned quickly that being an "introverted" waitress wasn't going to work. If I didn't smile at the customers, they thought I was unfriendly. If I didn't greet them enthusiastically, they didn't feel welcome or appreciated. If I didn't remember the names of the regular customers and what they liked to drink, they often wouldn't even leave me the change from their dollar.

I learned a lot of things during my years of waiting tables, off and on earlier in my career. You see the best and the worst of people when you wait tables. But, the most important lesson I learned was to take initiative and connect with my customers. **Communicating information wasn't enough. I had to connect with them.** I could tell them where to get a plate and take their drink order, but how I did it made all the difference in whether they left me anything at all, or sometimes, several dollars.

What I want to share with you in this book are some of the lessons I've learned about connecting with people and communicating effectively. There aren't any shortcuts to success, but I hope I can help you avoid the detours and map out a faster route.

Effective communication skills are critical to our success in life.

On the professional side, the ability to communicate and relate to customers, co-workers, employees, or your boss can determine your career potential and define your success.

On the personal side, communication with your spouse, children, parents, and friends will determine your satisfaction in life (at least some of it) and define your relationships.

Regardless of your preferred personality style, or whether you consider yourself an introvert or extrovert, dealing with other people is a fact of life. Almost any situation you can think of requires you to come in contact and interact with other people sooner or later.

Your eye color cannot be changed. Your genetic ability to run a four-minute mile cannot be changed. Your ability to communicate CAN be changed. **Communication is a skill anyone can learn, and everyone can learn to do it better.**

Excerpt from
Defining Influence:
Increasing Your Influence Increases Your Options
By Mack Story

In *Defining Influence*, I outline the foundational leadership principles and lessons we must learn in order to develop our character in a way that allows us to increase our influence with others. I also share many of my personal stories revealing how I got it wrong many times in the past and how I grew from front-line factory worker to become a Motivational Leadership Speaker.

INTRODUCTION

When You Increase Your Influence, You Increase Your Options.

"Leadership is influence. Nothing more. Nothing less. Everything rises and falls on leadership." ~ *John C. Maxwell*

Everyone is born a leader. However, everyone is not born a high impact leader.

I haven't always believed everyone is a leader. You may or may not at this point. That's okay. There is a lot to learn about leadership.

At this very moment, you may already be thinking to yourself, *"I'm not a leader."* My goal is to help you understand why everyone is a leader and to help you develop a deeper understanding of the principles of leadership and influence.

Developing a deep understanding of leadership has changed my life for the better. It has also changed the lives of my family members, friends, associates, and clients. My intention is to help you improve not only your life, but also the lives of those around you.

Until I became a student of leadership in 2008 which eventually led me to become a John C. Maxwell Certified Leadership Coach, Trainer, and Speaker in 2012, I did not understand leadership or realize everyone can benefit from learning the related principles.

In the past, I thought leadership was a term associated with being the boss and having formal authority over others. Those people are definitely leaders. But, I had been missing something. All of the other seven billion people on the planet are leaders too.

I say everyone is born a leader because I agree with John C. Maxwell, *"Leadership is Influence. Nothing more. Nothing less."* Everyone has influence. It's a fact. Therefore, everyone is a leader.

No matter your age, gender, religion, race, nationality, location, or position, everyone has influence. Whether you want to be a leader or not, you are. After reading this book, I hope you do not question whether or not you are a leader. However, I do hope you question what type of leader you are and what you need to do to increase your influence.

Everyone does not have authority, but everyone does have influence. There are plenty of examples in the world of people without authority leading people through influence alone. Actually, every one of us is an example. We have already done it. We know it is true. This principle is self-evident which means it contains its own evidence and does not need to be demonstrated or explained; it is obvious to everyone: we all have influence with others.

As I mentioned, the question to ask yourself is not, *"Am I a leader?"* The question to ask yourself is, *"What type of leader am I?"* The answer: whatever kind you choose to be. Choosing not to be a leader is not an option. As long as you live, you will have influence. You are a leader.

You started influencing your parents before you were actually born. You may have influence after your death. How? Thomas Edison still influences the world every time a light is turned on, you may do things in your life to influence others long after you're gone. Or, you may pass away with few people noticing. It depends on the choices you make.

Even when you're alone, you have influence.

The most important person you will ever influence is yourself. The degree to which you influence yourself determines the level of influence you ultimately have with others. Typically, when we are talking about leading ourselves, the word most commonly used to describe self-leadership is discipline which can be defined as giving yourself a command and following through with it. We must practice discipline daily to increase our influence with others.

"We must all suffer one of two things: the pain of discipline or the pain of regret or disappointment." ~ Jim Rohn

As I define leadership as influence, keep in mind the words leadership and influence can be interchanged anytime and anywhere. They are one and the same. Throughout this book, I'll help you remember by placing one of the words in parentheses next to the other occasionally as a reminder. They are synonyms. When you read one, think of the other.

Everything rises and falls on influence (leadership). When you share what you're learning, clearly define leadership as influence for others. They need to understand the context of what you are teaching and understand they *are* leaders (people with influence) too. If you truly want to learn and apply leadership principles, you must start teaching this material to others within 24-48 hours of learning it yourself.

You will learn the foundational principles of leadership (influence) which will help you understand the importance of the following five questions. You will be able to take effective action by growing yourself and possibly others to a higher level of leadership (influence). Everything you ever achieve, internally and externally, will be a direct result of your influence.

1. **Why do we influence?** – Our character determines *why* we influence. Who we are on the inside is what matters. Do we manipulate or motivate? It's all about our intent.

2. **How do we influence?** – Our character, combined with our competency, determines *how* we influence. Who we are and what we know combine to create our unique style of influence which determines our methods of influence.

3. **Where do we influence?** – Our passion and purpose determine *where* we have the greatest influence. What motivates and inspires us gives us the energy and authenticity to motivate and inspire others.

4. **Who do we influence?** – We influence those *who* buy-in to us. Only those valuing and seeking what we value and seek will volunteer to follow us. They give us or deny us permission to influence them based on how well we have developed our character and competency.

5. **When** do we influence? – We influence others *when* they want our influence. We choose when others influence us. Everyone else has the same choice. They decide when to accept or reject our influence.

The first three questions are about the choices we make as we lead (influence) ourselves and others. The last two questions deal more with the choices others will make as they decide first, *if* they will follow us, and second, *when* they will follow us. They will base their choices on *who we are* and *what we know.*

Asking these questions is important. Knowing the answers is more important. But, taking action based on the answers is most important. Cumulatively, the answers to these questions determine our leadership style and our level of influence (leadership).

On a scale of 1-10, your influence can be very low level (1) to very high level (10). But make no mistake, you *are* a leader. You *are* always on the scale. There is a positive and negative scale too. The higher on the scale you are the more effective you are. You will be at different levels with different people at different times depending on many different variables.

Someone thinking they are not a leader or someone that doesn't want to be a leader is still a leader. They will simply remain a low impact leader with low level influence getting low level results. They will likely spend much time frustrated with many areas of their life. Although they could influence a change, they choose instead to be primarily influenced by others.

What separates high impact leaders from low impact leaders? There are many things, but two primary differences are:

1) High impact leaders accept more responsibility in all areas of their lives while low impact leaders tend to blame others and transfer responsibility more often.

2) High impact leaders have more positive influence while low impact leaders tend to have more negative influence.

My passion has led me to grow into my purpose which is to help others increase their influence personally and professionally while setting and reaching their goals. I am very passionate and have great conviction. I have realized many benefits by getting better results in all areas of my life. I have improved relationships with my family members, my friends, my associates, my peers, and my clients. I have witnessed people within these same groups embrace leadership principles and reap the same benefits.

The degree to which I *live* what I teach determines my effectiveness. My goal is to learn it, live it, and *then* teach it. I had major internal struggles as I grew my way to where I am. I'm a long way from perfect, so I seek daily improvement. Too often, I see people teaching leadership but not living what they're teaching. If I teach it, I live it.

My goal is to be a better leader tomorrow than I am today. I simply must get out of my own way and lead. I must lead me effectively before I can lead others effectively, not only with acquired knowledge, but also with experience from applying and living the principles.

I'll be transparent with personal stories to help you see how I have applied leadership principles by sharing: How I've struggled. How I've learned. How I've sacrificed. And, how I've succeeded.

Go beyond highlighting or underlining key points. Take the time to write down your thoughts related to the principle. Write down what you want to change. Write down how you can apply the principle in your life. You may want to consider getting a journal to fully capture your thoughts as you progress through the chapters. What you are thinking as you read is often much more important than what you're reading.

Most importantly, do not focus your thoughts on others. Yes, they need it too. We all need it. I need it. You need it. However, if you focus outside of yourself, you are missing the very point. Your influence comes from within. Your influence rises and falls based on your choices. You have untapped and unlimited potential waiting to be released. Only you can release it.

You, like everyone else, were born a leader. Now, let's take a leadership journey together.

(If you enjoyed this Introduction to *Defining Influence*, it is available in paperback, audio, and as an eBook on Amazon.com)

ABOUT THE AUTHOR

Like many, Ria faced adversity in life. Ria was sexually abused by her father from age 12 - 19, forced to play the role of his wife, and even shared with other men. Desperate to escape, she left home at 19 without a job, a car, or even a high school diploma. Ria learned to be resilient, not only surviving, but thriving. She worked her way through college, earning her MBA with a cumulative 4.0 GPA, and had a successful career in the corporate world of administrative healthcare.

Ria's background includes more than 10 years in administrative healthcare including working as the Director of Compliance for a large healthcare organization. Ria's responsibilities included oversight of thousands of organizational policies, organizational compliance with all State and Federal regulations, and responsibility for several million dollars in Medicare appeals.

Today, Ria is a motivational leadership speaker, TEDx Speaker, and author of 14 books, including Leadership Gems for Women. Ria is a certified leadership speaker and trainer and was selected three times to speak on stage at International John C. Maxwell Certification Events. Motivational speaker Les Brown also invited Ria to share the stage with him in Los Angeles, CA.

Ria has a passion for health and wellness and is a certified group fitness instructor. She has completed several marathons and half-marathons and won both the Alabama and Georgia Women's State Mountain Biking Championships in 2011 and 2012.

Ria shares powerful leadership principles and tools of transformation from her journey to equip and empower women, helping them maximize their potential in life and leadership.

ABOUT MACK STORY

Mack's story is an amazing journey of personal and professional growth. He married Ria in 2001. He has one son, Eric, born in 1991.

After graduating high school in 1987, Mack joined the USMC Reserves as an 0311 infantryman. Soon after in 1988, he began his 20 plus year manufacturing career on the front lines of a large production machine shop. Graduating with highest honors, he earned an Executive Bachelor of Business Administration degree from Faulkner University in 2002. He eventually grew himself into upper management and found his niche in lean manufacturing and along with it, developed his passion for leadership. In 2008, he launched his own Lean Manufacturing and Leadership Development business.

From 2005-2012, Mack led leaders and their cross-functional teams through more than 11,000 hours of process improvement, organizational change, and cultural transformation. In 2013, Mack and Ria served with John C. Maxwell as part of Cultural Transformation in Guatemala where over 20,000 leaders were trained. They also shared the stage with internationally recognized motivational speaker Les Brown in 2014. In 2018, they were invited to speak at Yale University's School of Management.

Mack has also published 14 books on personal growth and leadership development including his five very popular *Blue-Collar Leadership® Series* books.

Mack and Ria inspire people everywhere through their example of achievement, growth, and personal development.

Clients: ATD (Association for Talent Development), Auburn University, Chevron, Chick-fil-A, Kimberly Clark, Koch Industries, Southern Company, and the U.S. Military.

Read more books by Ria

You have untapped potential to do, have, and be more in life. But, developing your potential and becoming the best version of yourself will require personal transformation. You will have to transform from who you are today into who you want to become tomorrow.

Ria Story brings unique insight in her book, "Fearfully and Wonderfully Me: Become the Woman You are Destined to Be" and the accompanying workbook to help you: believe in yourself and your potential; embrace your self-worth; overcome self-limiting beliefs; increase your influence personally & professionally; and achieve your goals & develop a mindset for success. These two resources will empower you to own your story, write a new chapter, and become the woman and leader you are destined to be.

Read more books by Ria

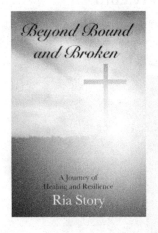

Ria Story

In *Beyond Bound and Broken*, Ria shares how she overcame the shame, fear, and doubt she developed after enduring years of extreme sexual abuse by her father. Forced to play the role of a wife and even shared with other men due to her father's perversions, Ria left home at 19 without a job, a car, or even a high-school diploma. This book also contains lessons on resilience and overcoming adversity that you can apply to your own life.

In *Ria's Story From Ashes To Beauty*, Ria tells her personal story of growing up as a victim of extreme sexual abuse from age 12 – 19, leaving home to escape, and her decision to tell her story.

Order books online at Amazon or RiaStory.com

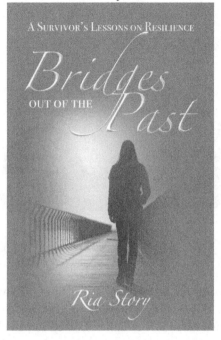

It's not what happens to you in life. It's who you become because of it. We all experience pain, grief, and loss in life. Resilience is the difference between *"I didn't die,"* and *"I learned to live again."* In this captivating book on resilience, Ria walks you through her own horrific story of more than seven years of sexual abuse by her father. She then shares how she learned not only to survive, but also to thrive in spite of her past. Learn how to overcome challenges, obstacles, and adversity in your own life by building a bridge out of the past and into the future.

(Watch 7 minutes of her story at RiaStory.com/TEDx)

Order books online at Amazon or RiaStory.com

Note: Leadership Gems is the generic, non-gender specific, version of Leadership Gems for Women. The content is very similar.

Women are naturally high impact leaders because they are relationship oriented. However, it's a *"man's world"* out there and natural ability isn't enough to help you be successful as a leader. You must be intentional.

Ria packed these books with 30 leadership gems which very successful people internalize and apply. Ria has combined her years of experience in leadership roles of different organizations along with years of studying, teaching, training, and speaking on leadership to give you these 30, short and simple, yet powerful and profound, lessons to help you become very successful, regardless of whether you are in a formal leadership position or not.

Order books online at Amazon or RiaStory.com

You have hopes, dreams, and goals you want to achieve. You have aspirations of leaving a legacy of significance. You have untapped potential waiting to be unleashed. But, unfortunately, how to maximize your potential isn't something addressed in job or skills training. And sadly, how to achieve success and find significance in life isn't something taught in school, college, or by most parents.

In *ACHIEVE: Maximize Your Potential with 7 Keys to Unlock Success and Significance*, Ria shares lessons to help you become more influential, more successful and maximize your potential in life. Three-page chapters are short, yet powerful, and provide principles on realizing your potential with actionable takeaways. These brief vignettes provide humorous, touching, or sad lessons straight from the heart that you can immediately apply to your own situation.

Motivational Planning Journals
Choose a theme for the season of your life!
Now available at Amazon.com or RiaStory.com

| Motivational | Purposeful/Living Your Legacy | Productivity |
| Joy/Faith | Resilience | Make the Most of Today |

Start each day with a purposeful mindset, and you will achieve your priorities based on your values.

Just a few minutes of intentional thought every morning will allow you to focus your energy, increase your influence, and make your day all that it can be!

Each journal in the series has different motivational quotes and a motivational theme. Choose one or get all six for an entire year's worth of **Motivational Planning**!

Order books online at Amazon or RiaStory.com

Become inspired by this 30-day collection of daily devotions for women, where you will find practical advice on intentionally living with a grateful heart, inspirational quotes, short journaling opportunities, and scripture from God's Word on practicing gratitude.

Order books online at Amazon or
RiaStory.com

Ria's *Effective Leadership Series* books are written to develop and enhance your leadership skills, while also helping you increase your abilities in areas like communication and relationships, time management, planning and execution, leading and implementing change. Look for more books in the *Effective Leadership Series*:

- *Straight Talk: The Power of Effective Communication*

- *PRIME Time: The Power of Effective Planning*

- *Change Happens: Leading Yourself and Others through Change (Co-authored by Ria & Mack Story)*

- *Leadership Gems & Leadership Gems for Women*

Read books by Mack Story

High impact leaders align their habits with key values in order to maximize their influence. High impact leaders intentionally grow and develop themselves in an effort to more effectively grow and develop others. These *10 Values* are commonly understood. However, they are not always commonly practiced. These *10 Values* will help you build trust and accelerate relationship building. Those mastering these *10 Values* will be able to lead with speed as they develop 360° of influence from wherever they are.

Order books online at Amazon or
TopStoryLeadership.com

Are you looking for transformation in your life? Do you want better results? Do you want stronger relationships?

In *Defining Influence*, Mack breaks down many of the principles that will allow anyone at any level to methodically and intentionally increase their positive influence.

Mack blends his personal growth journey with lessons on the principles he learned along the way. He's not telling you what he learned after years of research, but rather what he learned from years of application and transformation. Everything rises and falls on influence.

Order books online at Amazon or TopStoryLeadership.com

10 Foundational Elements of Intentional Transformation serves as a source of motivation and inspiration to help you climb your way to the next level and beyond as you learn to intentionally create a better future for yourself. The pages will ENCOURAGE, ENGAGE, and EMPOWER you as you become more focused and intentional about moving from where you are to where you want to be.

All of us are somewhere, but most of us want to be somewhere else. However, we don't always know how to get there. You will learn how to intentionally move forward as you learn to navigate the 10 foundational layers of transformation.

Order books online at Amazon or TopStoryLeadership.com

"Sales persuasion and influence, moving others, has changed more in the last 10 years than it has in the last 100 years. It has transitioned from buyer beware to seller beware" ~ *Daniel Pink*

So, it's no longer *"Buyer beware!"* It's *"Seller beware!"* Why? Today, the buyer has the advantage over the seller. Most often, they are holding it in their hand. It's a smart phone. They can learn everything about your product before they meet you. They can compare features and prices instantly. The major advantage you do still have is: YOU! IF they like you. IF they trust you. IF they feel you want to help them. This book is filled with 30 short chapters providing unique insights that will give you the advantage, not over the buyer, but over your competition: those who are selling what you're selling. It will help you sell yourself.

Order books online at Amazon or TopStoryLeadership.com

It's easier to compete when you're attracting great people instead of searching for good people. *Blue-Collar Leadership® & Culture* will help you understand why culture is the key to becoming a sought after employer of choice within your industry and in your area of operation.

You'll also discover how to leverage the components of The Transformation Equation to create a culture that will support, attract, and retain high performance team members.
Blue-Collar Leadership® & Culture is intended to serve as a tool, a guide, and a transformational road map for leaders who want to create a high impact culture that will become their greatest competitive advantage

Order books online at Amazon or BlueCollarLeadership.com

Are you ready to play at the next level and beyond?

In today's high stakes game of business, the players on the team are the competitive advantage for any organization. But, only if they are on the field instead of on the bench.

The competitive advantage for every individual is developing 360° of influence regardless of position, title, or rank.

Blue-Collar Leadership® & *Teamwork* provides a simple, yet powerful and unique, resource for individuals who want to increase their influence and make a high impact. It's also a resource and tool for leaders, teams, and organizations, who are ready to Engage the Front Line to Improve the Bottom Line.

Order books online at Amazon or BlueCollarLeadership.com

Fast and Effective Workforce & Leadership Development for Team Members and Leaders at Every Level

Leaders are **BUSY**. The greatest challenge High Impact leaders face in leadership development is the struggle to find <u>time.</u>

Workforce development is **critical** for creating a leadership culture that attracts, retains, and engages top talent. Unfortunately however, opportunities for growth, team building, and leadership development are often pushed aside, second to project deadlines, customer needs, and urgent job details.

That's why Mack Story designed *Toolbox Tips*, a collection of powerful leadership principles delivered in a short and easy to understand format for quick and *consistent* workforce development.

Order books online at Amazon or BlueCollarLeadership.com

"I wish someone had given me these books 30 years ago when I started my career on the front lines. They would have changed my life then. They can change your life now." ~ Mack Story

Blue-Collar Leadership® *& Supervision* and *Blue-Collar Leadership*® are written specifically for those who lead the people on the frontlines and for those on the front lines. With 30 short, easy to read 3 page chapters, these books contain powerful, yet simple to understand leadership lessons.

Download the first 5 chapters of each book FREE at: BlueCollarLeadership.com/download

Order books online at Amazon or TopStoryLeadership.com

"I wish someone had given me these books 30 years ago when I started my career. They would have changed my life then. They can change your life now." ~ Mack Story

MAXIMIZE Your Potential will help you learn to lead yourself well. *MAXIMIZE Your Leadership Potential* will help you learn to lead others well. With 30 short, easy to read 3 page chapters, these books contain simple and easy to understand, yet powerful leadership lessons.

Note: These two MAXIMIZE books are the white-collar, or non-specific, version of the Blue-Collar Leadership® books and contain nearly identical content.

Special Offer!

FOR A LIMITED TIME, Ria is offering a special speaking or training package. Take advantage of the special offer with a reduced speaking/training fee of only $5,400 and receive:

- Up to 2 hours of on-site speaking or training
- 300 copies of one or more of her books FREE!
- For details, topics, and programs visit: RiaStory.com/SpecialOffer

Call today! Deals like this don't last forever! 334.332.3526 or visit RiaStory.com

"My first words are, GET SIGNED UP! This training is not, and I stress, not your everyday leadership seminar...nothing can touch what Mack and Ria Story provide!"

~ Sam McLamb, VP & COO

334.332.3526
Ria@RiaStory.com